OUT OF CHINA, WITH CHRIST

OUT OF CHINA, WITH CHRIST

ROLAND MULLER

Out of China, with Christ

Copyright © 2026 by Roland Muller

All rights reserved. No part of this book may be reproduced in any manner whatsoever without written permission except in the case of brief quotations embodied in critical articles and reviews.

Previous parts of this book have been published in electronic format under the titles *Companion Reader Two* and *Companion Reader Three* by Roland Muller.

First Printing, 2026

ISBN 978-1-927581-30-8

INTRODUCTION
1

MISSIONARY STORY ONE
6

MISSIONARY STORY TWO
153

Introduction

Starting in the 1920s in Shangdong Province (Shaanxi) in China, members of the Jesus Generation (also known as the Jesus Family) studied the Bible together and grew in their faith. They believed that the ultimate act of faith was to sell their possessions and distribute them among others in greater need. Their five word slogan described their commitment to Christ and their simple lifestyle: *Sacrifice, Abandonment, Poverty, Suffering and Death*. Groups of the Jesus Generation walked from one place to another, preaching the gospel as they met people. Their commitment to communal life and helping one another impressed many who met them. As they spread the gospel, their small beginnings turned into a movement. Not only did thousands join them, but many blind people, beggars, homeless and destitute thronged to them, becoming part of these moving communities of believers as they walked from village to village.

But there were huge challenges. It wasn't long before the word went before them, and entire towns turned out to beat them and humiliate them. But this opposition did not deter them. Everywhere they traveled, there were a few people who were willing to forsake all and follow Jesus.

Twenty years later, there were more than 20,000 believers in more than 100 different Jesus Generation groups. In Fengxiang, Shaanxi Province, the Northwest Missionary School was started. On Easter Sunday, April 25, 1943, eleven students at the school shared with one another how the Lord had called each to take the gospel to Xinjiang and beyond.

Vice-Principle Mark Ma Peixuan encouraged the students to adopt a Chinese name from Matthew 24:14 that literally meant "The Preach the Gospel Everywhere Band." However, they came to be known in English by the name used by their missionary colleagues, the Back to Jerusalem Evangelistic Band. Their dream was to take their small marching community preaching the gospel from China, across the Muslim world, all the way to Jerusalem. It was their belief that the Gospel started in Jerusalem and had traveled all the way around the world until it reached China. Now it was their mission to complete the circle and take the gospel through Buddhist, Hindu and Muslim lands. Pastor Ma challenged his students to consider first taking the gospel outside of China to the area known today as Kazakhstan.

In March 1947, six missionaries left Fengxiang for the long journey to Xinjiang. Of the four women in the group, one was married and with child, and three were single. Another lady, Grace, worked hard to support them. She lived until her 90s, totally focused on praying and supporting missionaries. All six, led by Simon Zhao Ximen, the husband of the pregnant woman, headed for Kashgar in the Xinjiang region of north-west China. They walked many days, preaching the gospel in the towns and villages as they traveled towards the border. After 300 miles of walking, they reached Xinjiang, the capital of Qinghai where they were joined by a seventh member who was waiting for them. There they applied for permission to enter the Soviet Union.

As the group waited for the needed papers, communist armies under Chairman Mao took control of Xinjiang. The communists sealed the borders to keep anyone from fleeing China. All missionaries, including Simon's team, were imprisoned. Of his missionary team, only Simon survived imprisonment.

He and his wife, Wen Muling, had arrived in Xinjiang in 1949 after walking most of the way from eastern China. They had been married less than a year when they were arrested in January 1950. Simon saw Muling through iron bars twice shortly after their arrest and then never again on this earth. She was at that time pregnant with their first child but miscarried and died in prison in 1959. Simon and the others endured years of beatings and were forced to work long, hard hours, with insufficient food and care. One by one, they died. All except Simon Zhao.

Each evening Simon would face towards the west and cry out to God. His heart burned to walk across the Muslim world, preaching the gospel until he would arrive in Jerusalem. Not just him alone, but others with him who had decided to follow Jesus—a moving, growing community of believers marching and preaching. The walls of the prison and the endless beatings could not squelch his vision.

In 1981 Simon Zhao was unexpectedly released from prison after 31 years incarcerated. No one even knew he was still alive. Debra Su, a Christian lady who spoke to him some time later, discovered that when we was released he hadn't heard of the cultural revolution and he hadn't heard of Mao Tse Tung. He had missed all of it.

He emerged from prison beaten and abused for 31 years, but God had preserved his life. He didn't know where to go or what to do so he built a little hut on the outer perimeter of the prison waiting to see what God had for him next. One day, he was singing in his little hut when some Christian ladies from the nearby city of Kashgar passed by. They heard the singing and wondered who it might be. They turned aside to see who was singing, and they discovered that Simon Zhao had been released. Quickly, word spread across China, and eventually it came to Hunan Province. By the middle of the 1980s, the house church movement had become very strong, especially in the Wenzhou area of Hunan, after a powerful Christian revival movement.

The government Three Self Church has grown from 9 million to 16 million in recent years. Those are the official figures of the state approved church. Some have suggested that the house churches number around 85 million. 100 million may sound phenomenal, but the gospel has not reached all of China. 100 million Christians is around 7% of China's population. The majority of Christians in China are ethnically are Han Chinese, but there are many unreached people groups within China. For instance, China has the second largest Muslim population in the world, second only to Indonesia. In recent years, the province of Yunan experienced a revival, but it is also one of the toughest areas in China right now. Some have suggested that 25,000 people are coming to Christ each day in China.

But back in 1981, unnoticed by the world, Simon Zhao was released from prison. As news of his release spread across the church in China, Debra Su (Xu Yongling) heard the news and traveled seven days by train to meet him. She had been in and out of prison for many years herself. When she finally reached him, she asked him to return with her to Hunan. After 31 years in prison and endless beatings, he replied to Debra, "how can I go eastwards when God has called me to go west?"

As she prayed, Debra received a word of wisdom from God and she said to Simon Zhao, "if you will come back to Hunan, it won't be just one man going, it will be many going, because as you tell your story, many will be inspired. Please come back and raise an army that will go westwards."

So, Simon Zhao went back to Hunan. He lived there from 1989 until he went to be with the Lord in 2001, but for 12 years he travelled and spoke in many small house-churches. And so, the vision to take the gospel across the Muslim world began with Mark Ma and his students, and then it passed to Simon Zhao. For 31 years the vision was dead. The marching communities of the Jesus Generation ended under communism, but the house churches grew while they suffered persecution. God used Simon Zhao to spread the missionary vision among the believers in China and now that vision has borne fruit. All over China, the church began to speak in terms of reaching the House of Islam, the House of Hinduism, and the house of Buddha.

While this all sounds exciting and even exhilarating, the challenges are vast. Most people in the house churches in China are poor. Many have limited education and few resources. Yet they have zeal and a willingness to sacrifice and push forward. In recent years, small Bible Schools and training centers have sprung up across China, seeking to better educate those who are coming forward to answer the missionary call. Many of these are not volunteers, but are chosen by their house church to go and finish the job of evangelizing the world.

EXPLANATION

With this background in mind, this book contains two stories. Are they fiction or truth? The main characters in each story are fiction, but the situations they faced are drawn from true events. So these stories are a blend of fiction and truth. My wife and I either experienced situations like these ourselves, or heard them from others whom we knew dealt with these same issues. I share these with you to encourage you and help you understand the challenges that missionaries face in sharing the gospel with Muslims.

The first story is the account of Mr. Li, who travels from China to a Middle Eastern country. To support himself, he takes a job supervising cleaners in a city hospital. From this lowly position, he desires to see Muslims won for Christ. The second story is of a Chinese couple with a young son who travel to a central Asian city with the dream of starting a group of believers there.

In these stories I attempt to use real-life situations, drawn from over 40 years of missionary service to Muslims, to help you, the reader, understand the challenges and opportunities that exist in ministry to Muslims. I trust God will challenge you to become involved in taking the gospel to those near you who need to hear. I trust you will not only enjoy these stories, but through them you will learn something.

Roland Muller
WEC International
2026

Missionary Story One

1

Mr. Li had only recently arrived in the Middle East from China. He was excited to be there and looked forward to sharing Jesus with Muslim people. But the culture and the people were all very strange to him, and he spent the first few weeks simply adjusting to his new surroundings. He was surprised to discover how hot it was during the summer, with daytime temperatures rising to over 40 degrees Celsius. Thankfully, the weather cooled off in the evening, so he could sleep very comfortably. People told him that during the winter he should expect cold, rain, and perhaps snow. It was hard for him to believe since the summer was so warm.

Mr. L worked in a hospital, overseeing the sweepers and cleaners. All of the cleaners were Muslims, most of them from other countries. Many of the cleaners were from very poor backgrounds and were not very clean themselves. Mr. Li had to work hard to monitor their work and encourage them to do a good job.

Mr. Li had come to the Middle East with a desire to share the gospel with Muslim people. Each morning he would meet with the sweepers and assign them their cleaning duties. Before he assigned their duties, using his broken English, Mr. Li would welcome them to work that morning, and then tell them that he had a word of wisdom for the day. Usually, he chose to share something from the teachings of Jesus. Most of them didn't know much English, and Mr. Li didn't know the local language, so the cleaners would sit quietly while he read a Bible verse to them.

Mr. Li tried to encourage them in their work and attitudes. Mr. Li did the best he could within the scope of his official work in the country, but his heart's desire was to witness to the local people and plant a church among them. The problem was Mr. Li lived in the hospital compound with other Asians. It was quite hard to meet any local people. Then God opened a door of opportunity for Mr. Li.

One day, one of the western doctors in the hospital who was also a believer, Dr. Wilson, stopped Mr. Li in a hallway. Dr. Wilson had noticed Mr. Li's Bible and recognized him as a Christian, but the two seldom saw each other at the hospital. The doctor asked Mr. Li if he would like to accompany him on a visit to one of the local leaders. Mr. Li's heart was filled with thankfulness. Finally, God was opening a door of opportunity for him, and he graciously accepted Dr. Wilson's invitation.

That evening, Dr. Wilson took Mr. Li in his car and drove across town to where the local leader, or Sheik, lived. They drove into the more modern area of the city and parked the car in front of a large building with a small garden in front of it. Together, they walked up to the front door and rang the bell. A young man met them at the door and welcomed them. As they entered the house, they removed their shoes, and stepped onto a very expensive-looking Persian carpet. They were shown into a very long room with large chairs ornately carved from wood. After a few minutes, the local ruler and another man entered the room. Both were dressed in western business suits.

Mr. Li and Dr. Wilson rose to their feet. The two Arab men shook the doctor's hand and then Mr. Li's. Despite the handshake, they barely seemed to notice Mr. Li. They sat for a few minutes and the doctor exchanged greetings with the Sheik, asking him how he was, how his family was, and about the hospital. The Sheik and doctor Wilson seemed to be well acquainted.

After a few minutes of small talk, a young man came to the door and announced that the food was ready. They rose, and the Sheik motioned them towards the door. Dr. Wilson indicated that the Sheik should go first. The Sheik insisted that the doctor should go first. In the end, Dr. Wilson accepted and turned to the door. Mr. Li quietly followed. They entered into another room where they sat on the floor before a low table covered with many different kinds of food and drink. Then another young man entered with a large bowl of warm water and a towel. The doctor dipped his right hand into a large bowl of hot water and then dried it on the towel. Mr. Li was unsure what to do, so he did just as the doctor had done. The Sheik and the other Arab man also washed their right hands and then indicated that they should eat.

On the table was a very large plate with a huge pile of rice, crowned with pieces of meat. The host poured a creamy white liquid over the rice and indicated that they should start. Mr. Li watched curiously as the Sheik and his friend moved around the other side of the table and placed their hands directly into the plate of rice, taking a handful of rice and liquid, squeezing them to form a lump. Then they flipped the balls of rice into their mouths using their thumbs. The doctor tried it but was having a hard time. Mr. Li decided he should try. Placing his hand into the food, he discovered that it was quite hot. He tried squeezing the rice but it just came out between his fingers. The Arab men were smiling, and someone offered Dr. Wilson a spoon. He shook his head and tried harder.

"Look," the Sheik smiled. "Try this."

He then ripped off a small piece of flat bread and used it to pinch the food. Mr. Li followed, and this time was successful. The food had a strong, rather sour taste. Then the men dug their hands in again, mixing it with small pieces of meat they ripped off with their hands. Mr. Li recognized the meat as sheep meat. The large platter contained ribs with meat attached to them.

Their Sheik continued to eat as long as his guests were eating. After a while, the doctor stopped eating. Mr. Li also stopped, wanting to be courteous. When they were all done, the Sheik called out and the young man entered the room with more warm water and another towel. They each washed their right hands and then dried them on the towel. Then they moved back into the sitting room.

As Mr. Li sat in a large, uncomfortable chair, he wondered what he should say to his host. He silently prayed, unsure how he could even speak to such a wealthy man. He knew nothing of what this man faced each day. How could he, a lowly worker, say anything that this man would even consider interesting?

He didn't have time to think and pray any further: he heard the Sheik ask Dr. Wilson about Mr. Li.

"Where is this man from?"

"My friend, Mr. Li, is from China. He works at the hospital."

"Oh, China." The Sheik smiled and turned to Mr. Li. "Are you a Muslim?"

Mr. Li was surprised at the direct question. "No," he said. "I am not."

"That's too bad," the Sheik said. "You must not have heard about our great religion. I am sure once you hear, you will be happy to become a Muslim."

Mr. Li stared. He didn't know what to say.

"Let me tell you about our prophet," the Sheik continued. "He was the greatest man that ever lived. God sent him to be a prophet to all people, and through him, God revealed his word, the Qur'an. This is God's message to all mankind." The Sheik smiled warmly at Mr. Li. "Do you have a Qur'an?"

Mr. Li was again unsure how to answer. "No," he said truthfully. "I do not."

"I will get you one." The Sheik was now excited. "What language would you like it in?" He paused. "The Qur'an is always in Arabic, but it is now being made available with different languages that accompany the Arabic. Would you like English or Chinese? I have English ones here in the house."

Mr. Li did not know what to do. He did not want to refuse his host. He really didn't want a Qur'an. "English is fine," he managed to say.

The Sheik smiled again and began talking about the glorious religion of Islam and how it unites all men together as brothers.

Dr. Wilson tried to join the conversation, but he never managed to counter the Sheik's comments. After an hour the doctor began to prepare to leave.

As they rose, the Sheik smiled and told them, "I'm so glad that both of you have come to our country. In your countries, you did not have a chance to see the glories of Islam first-hand. Here you will be able to see how wonderful our society is, and experience Islam for yourselves. I'm sure that given time, you will have to agree with me that Islam is the most wonderful religion on earth." He shook Mr. Li's hand. "There are a few Muslims in your country but, in-sha-allah, some day all of your countrymen will recognize the superiority of Islam and the truths in our glorious Qur'an." At that point the young man appeared at the door with a Qur'an in his hands. He reverently placed it into Mr. Li's hands as they departed.

Once he was home, Mr. Li had time to think about the visit. He had come to this country as a messenger, but he was starting to understand that the local people did not want to hear anything he had to say. They did not consider him to be a messenger. In fact, the opposite was true. They believed that they had the true religion and that Mr. Li needed to convert to their religion. How was he, a foreigner, going to share Christ with these people? Even Dr. Wilson hadn't been able to say anything. How was he, a mere sweeper, going to win Muslims to Christ?

2

After his visit to the Sheik's house, Mr. Li was very discouraged. Back in his home country he had been regarded in the church as someone who was able to share his faith with others. People knew him and respected him. But here he was a stranger, just another Asian worker who walked past people on the street without being greeted.

As Mr. Li prayed about what he should do, he felt the Lord directing him to learn the local language. One of the men on his cleaning crew, Ahmed, was from a neighboring country, but could speak the language. So, the next day Mr. Li approached him and asked Ahmed if he would help him. At first Ahmed was very reluctant. How could he teach? He was only a sweeper.

"May I ask you questions?" Mr. Li asked. "For example, what is this?" He held up a pen. The man brightened. "That is a *gulum hibr*."

"See," Mr. Li smiled. "That wasn't so hard."

That afternoon, Mr. Li asked about several items and learned ten new words which he wrote down. All of them were the names of common things: a door, a window, paper, a pencil, a book, and so on. He worked hard that night to memorize these news words, and the next morning he asked Ahmed to test him.

Mr. Li didn't do very well. Yes, he knew the names, but he had trouble pronouncing the names correctly. So during the day, whenever he had a chance, he would take out his paper and go over the list. That night he obtained ten new words and memorized them. It was going to be hard work, but he had made a start. Mr. Li figured that if he memorized 1000 words, he would be able to talk to anyone. If he learned ten new words every day, he would reach his goal of a thousand words in three months. Then he might try sharing something of the gospel with the sweepers and cleaners with whom he worked.

At the end of three months, Mr. Li was very much encouraged. Everyone seemed pleased to be helping him, and he was now putting simple sentences together. This enabled him to go shopping and order meals at a nearby eatery. While he enjoyed the rice and bean meals, he was struggling to enjoy eating bread every day for breakfast and lunch. But Mr. Li was determined to become a part of the community that he lived in, and that included eating local food.

Sharing the gospel, however, was much more difficult. Mr. Li realized that he didn't have the right words to use. One night, he had an opportunity to share with Ahmed a little about his religion. He tried explaining that his holy book was the Bible, and that God spoke to him as he read. Ahmed looked very puzzled.

"God speaks to you?" he asked, shaking his head. "How is this possible?" Ahmed looked very concerned. "Mr. Li, do you hear voices?"

Mr. Li was alarmed. "No," he said. "I don't hear voices. As I read, God speaks to me."

Ahmed shook his head. "No," he insisted. "Muhammad was the last prophet. He heard God's voice. Only prophets heard God speak, and our prophet was the last one to hear God speak. It cannot be."

As Ahmed left, Mr. Li was very disappointed. How was he going to share the gospel? He didn't know where to start. That night, Mr. Li poured out his heart to God. He had worked hard to start learning the language, but now even that didn't seem to help much. Despite the setback, Mr. Li recommitted himself to learn more of the language. He needed to learn to express himself better, and he needed to learn the Muslim religious words.

The next week as Mr. Li was working around the hospital, he noticed a young western man sitting in a courtyard, reading a book. As Mr. Li walked past him, he recognized that the book was the Bible. After finishing his errand, Mr. Li returned and saw the same young man still sitting there. Mr. Li approached him and smiled. The young man looked up and also smiled.

"Bible?" Mr. Li asked.

"Yes," the young man smiled. "Are you a Christian?"

Mr. Li nodded. "Are you?" he asked back, in his best English.

The young man's smile broadened. "Yes," he said. "Sit down."

Mr. Li was overwhelmed with joy at meeting another believer. He sat down and together they tried to communicate with one another. The young man's name was David. He was from America.

"I am from China," Mr. Li said proudly. "I have come here to tell people about Jesus."

David looked worried and glanced around him nervously. "Not so loud," he said. "Someone might hear you."

Mr. Li was puzzled. Everyone in the hospital knew he was a Christian. Why was this brother so worried? They continued to speak in hushed tones. Mr. Li explained that he was learning the language, but was still struggling with communicating with people about Christ.

"Can you help me know how to tell people about Jesus?" he asked David.

"Sure" David said, "I can help you." He took a small yellow booklet from his pocket. "I use this book; it is called the *Four Spiritual Laws*. I was training in using this back home in America." He handed it to Mr. Li. "Here, you can have this one. I have lots more."

Mr. Li was very happy to have a tool which he could use to share Christ. After their visit, David and Mr. Li decided to meet in three days' time in the same courtyard.

That evening, Mr. Li read through the small booklet. "*Yes,*" he thought. "*I will try and use this with Ahmed and see if he understands the gospel better.*"

Several days later, Ahmed and several other sweepers were sitting around their small workroom and the discussion turned to religion. The men proudly explained to Mr. Li that they prayed five times a day. "Do you pray?" one of them asked.

"Yes!" Mr. Li was happy to have a chance to talk about his faith. "I pray many times a day."

"Really?" they said. "We don't see you pray."

"I pray every morning and evening, and also while I am walking around the hospital."

The men started laughing.

"What's so funny?" Mr. Li asked.

"When we pray, we face the Holy city of Mecca, and bow down. How can you do that walking around?" they laughed.

"Oh," Mr. Li said. "I don't do formal prayers like you do. I just talk to God."

"You talk to God?" they asked.

"And he hears God talk to him!" Ahmed added.

The men all turned directly toward Mr. Li. "Do you hear voices?" one of them asked in amazement.

Mr. Li shook his head. "It's more than that. If you would like to learn about my religion, I would be happy to tell you."

"Sure," one of them said. "Let's learn about Chinese religion."

"This isn't Chinese religion," Mr. Li said. "I follow Jesus. It's all written in my Holy books, the Bible."

"Okay," another of them said. "Tell us about your religion."

Mr. Li took out the small yellow booklet that David had given him. He opened to the first page and read: "God loves you and offers a wonderful plan for your life." Then he read John 3:16: "For God so loved the world that he gave his only begotten Son, that whosoever believes..."

"Stop," the men said. "God does not have a son. You speak blasphemy!"

Mr. Li looked up, startled by their anger.

"God is one" they said. "God is complete."

"God does not take or give in marriage," another insisted.

"God did not have a son" another shouted, and they started talking so fast that Mr. Li could not follow what they were saying. After a few minutes the angry men left. Mr. Li looked at the small yellow booklet. It had been no help at all. In fact, it had only made his friends angry.

When Mr. Li stopped for his afternoon break, a message was waiting for him. "You are wanted in the director's office at 4:00." Mr. Li frowned. He wondered what the message could be about.

He quickly drank his tea and then made his way through the hospital to the director's office. The secretary outside asked him to sit in the waiting room. After a long wait, she came and asked him to follow her. A few moments later she showed him into a large office. The director was sitting behind his large desk, apparently hard at work. Then he looked up.

"Mr. Li, I have been reading the reports we have about your work. You are a good worker. For the first time in a long time the sweepers are working well, and the hospital is clean. You have done a good job." He paused. "However, I have heard reports that you are preaching your religion all over the hospital. This will not do. This is your place of work, not a place of preaching." The director looked stern. "Mr. Li, we in this country are Muslims. We follow the true religion. Some day you may come to accept Islam as the true way." He paused again. "Mr. Li, I am responsible for the people who work in my hospital. We have many good Muslims here, and I am responsible for them. Mr. Li, those who do not follow Islam are going to hell. It is my duty to protect my workers. Yes, I am responsible for even their very souls, as long as they are working here for me. So I ask you, please refrain from preaching your religion here in this hospital. You are here to work, not preach. If you insist on preaching, I will have you thrown out of this country and sent back to China."

He stood and frowned at Mr. Li. "If you want to be a Christian, you can be a Christian. This is a free country. But you are not allowed to preach your religion here. This is a place of work, not a place of preaching." He picked up a sheet of paper. "I am going to be watching you very closely. If I see another report about you preaching, I will take action." He paused. "You can go now, but no more preaching."

Mr. Li turned and left. He didn't know what to say. Back in his room, he threw himself onto his bed and then slipped to his knees. Pouring out his heart to God, he sobbed and asked God to forgive him for being failure. He had come to this Muslim country to preach Christ, and now he was forbidden to do so. How would he ever win a Muslim to Christ? How would he ever start a church?

3

Several days later, Mr. Li met David in one of the hospital courtyards. David smiled and motioned for Mr. Li to sit beside him. "So how is it going?" he asked. "Did you get a chance to use the *Four Spiritual Laws* book I gave you?"

Mr. Li looked down. He was embarrassed to say anything, but he wanted to be honest with his friend. "Perhaps I didn't really understand how to use it," he began. David waited for him to continue. "I tried using it with some of the men in my crew. When I read John 3:16 to them, they became very angry. They were upset that the verse said that God had a son."

"I guess that makes sense," David said slowly.

Mr. Li looked up. "What happens when you use it?"

It was David's turn to look embarrassed. "Actually," he admitted. "I have never really used it here, only at home in America."

"Do Americans get upset when you say God had a son?"

"No, most don't really care much about God and religion."

"So you haven't used *The Four Spiritual Laws* with a Muslim?"

"No," David paused. "Look, I'm sorry about this. I just thought that whatever worked at home would work here." He paused. "Were the men really angry?"

"Yes, for a while they were, but they seemed to calm down. Things went okay after that until I was called into the director's office."

"Uh oh."

"He was very upset and threatened to send me back to China if I 'preached' again. I don't know what he meant by preaching. All I did was read one Bible verse to the men."

"I'm very sorry," David said. "I was only trying to help."

The two men sat quietly in the courtyard, not saying much after that. Then David brightened. "I think you went too fast. Maybe the men were not ready for the Bible yet. Perhaps they needed some Friendship Evangelism first."

Mr. Li was puzzled. "What is Friendship Evangelism?" he asked.

"Oh, that's when you make friends with someone and concentrate on the relationship. It takes time, but you become really close to someone. Then you look for opportunities to say things about the Bible and stuff. If you are a good friend, they don't become so angry."

"It sounds like it takes a long time."

"Yes, but this is what all the missionaries are doing now. It takes time, but when you have good friends, they don't get angry, and you can share more of the gospel."

"Do you have Muslim friends that you are doing this with?"

"Yes, I've been building friendships with three people. My landlord, his son, and a young man I met in the market."

"So, what sort of things do you do?"

"Well, I visit them, drink tea with them, and talk."

"What do you talk about?"

"Whatever they want to talk about. We're just friends. Sometimes I help them with English; sometimes they help me with the local language." David paused. "Look, it's easy. Everyone is doing it. Just relax and build friendships with a few people, and God will provide you with opportunities to share something someday."

As the two of them parted, David encouraged Mr. Li not to rush, but to take time and build relationships.

Several months later, Mr. Li was much more relaxed in his workplace. He no longer read a scripture verse with the men in the morning. He was no longer plagued with thoughts about how to evangelize Muslims. Since Mr. Li was no longer talking about religion, Ahmed seemed to have warmed up to him more, and their relationship was deepening. The director was much happier with Mr. Li as well. He would sometimes acknowledge him in the hallways and was always friendly with him. Mr. Li was also improving his language skills. He could join the different circles of people in the hospital and talk with them on many subjects. Mr. Li was now enjoying his life at the hospital. He could joke and talk with people without feeling pressured that he should be talking about God.

In fact, over the months, Mr. Li almost forgot about wanting to share the gospel. It started with his prayer life. Since he no longer felt pressured to share Christ, he no longer felt pressure to spend time in prayer each day. At first, it was only once that he missed his prayer time. He had slept in one morning because he had been out late the night before, drinking tea and talking with the men. He rushed to get into the workroom, and by the time his long workday had ended, he had few thoughts about God. That night he fell into his bed, tired, and ready to sleep. He turned over and closed his eyes, forgetting all about praying. The next day Mr. Li felt bad about missing his prayer time, but over the following weeks, it happened again, and then a third time. After a while, it was only a couple of days a week that he remembered to pray.

But on the other hand, his relationships were growing. One of the men who worked at the hospital, named Mustafa, invited him to his home, and soon he was a regular visitor there. On weekends, they would travel to a picnic spot in the country. Mr. Li enjoyed these visits very much. He enjoyed playing with Mustafa's children and talking about life in China. Mustafa was always interested in learning about China, its peoples, history, and accomplishments.

Mr. Li also continued to visit with David, although these visits became sporadic as both of them became more involved in the lives of people around them. In fact, they soon became quite busy, and their visits dropped off.

Sometime later, something happened while Mr. Li was visiting the local vegetable market. "You speak the local language," the merchant remarked with surprise.

"Just a little," Mr. Li responded meekly.

"No, you speak better than I speak," the merchant insisted.

"You are too kind," Mr. Li insisted, "I am only learning your language."

As he turned to go, a young man stepped up beside him. "Where are you from?" he asked him.

"I'm from China," Mr. Li said.

"China?" the young man said. "I've always been interested in China. How long have you been here?"

"About half a year." Mr. Li started to walk along the street towards his home.

"Do you live near here? I would like to visit you."

"I live up at the hospital workers' compound," Mr. Li replied.

As they walked along, the young man asked many more questions and Mr. Li began to think about Friendship Evangelism. Perhaps this was God's way of providing him with a new opportunity. As they talked, Mr. Li learned that the young man's name was Ramadan, the same name as the Muslim Holy month. Ramadan was from a nearby village and was in the city looking for work. When they reached the workers' compound, Ramadan continue to talk and follow him, so Mr. Li proceeded to his room. Ramadan seemed eager to see inside.

"So this is where you live. Do you live alone?"

"I have a room to myself, as I am the supervisor. The rest of the men sleep in that large room."

"Where is the bathroom?"

"We all share the toilet, and we share the shower as well."

"Is this your kitchen?"

"Yes, we make tea here, and sometimes cook something small. Most of us eat at the hospital."

Ramadan seemed genuinely interested in Mr. Li. They agreed to meet again the next afternoon.

The following afternoon, Ramadan showed up exactly as he promised. Mr. Li made him some tea, and they started to get to know one another. Ramadan came from a large family with many sisters and brothers. He also had many other relatives, as both his mother and father were from large families. Ramadan was in his early twenties. He was a Muslim, and his family were all Muslims. He was unemployed and looking for work. But work was hard to find. Most jobs paid too little. Ramadan was staying at a rooming-house in the center of town.

During their visit, Ramadan asked Mr. Li about China. Were the Chinese Muslims? Did Chinese drink whiskey or beer? He had heard that opium came from China. Had Mr. Li ever seen opium or hashish? Was it true that most young people in China were men? What would the Chinese do if there were not enough women to provide wives for all the men?

At the end of the visit, Mr. Li was very tired. These were hard questions to answer. He didn't really have the vocabulary to discuss them and sometimes didn't know how to answer these questions at all. They left him a bit disturbed.

On their third visit, Ramadan asked Mr. Li if he had any sisters. Ramadan was single and looking for a wife. He also asked Mr. Li if he would help him get a visa to China. At the end of the visit, Ramadan invited Mr. Li to visit his family in the village. This pleased Mr. Li, as he felt that a visit to a village would be very helpful, and he would get to know Ramadan better.

Ramadan continued to ask questions and seemed interested in everything that Mr. Li had in his room, except his Bible. Ramadan never asked any questions about this. Before they departed, Ramadan arranged that on Friday, the Muslim holy day, he would visit the village. Ramadan would come to his house at 8:00 in the morning and they would travel to the village.

On Friday, Mr. Li was up early to prepare to leave. Ramadan arrived and together they walked down the hill towards the center of the city. From there, they took a small bus to the edge of town where there was a very large bus station. Buses came from all over the country to this one point. Together, they boarded a bus that was going north and waited for the bus to fill up. After a half hour, the bus was finally full, and the driver got in. First, he collected the fares from everyone. Ramadan told Mr. Li how much the fares were, and Mr. Li paid for both of them. Ramadan never offered to pay, even for his own bus ride. After a few minutes the bus left. As they drove along, Ramadan pointed out various places and towns along the way.

The ride to the village took over an hour. Once they arrived in the village, Ramadan pointed the way and they walked along a narrow road. Then they turned into a path between fields. Although most of the grass was brown and the path was dry and dusty, it still reminded Mr. Li of his home. He felt strangely homesick.

Ramadan's home was a simple cement block house of two rooms. One room was for the women and the other room was for the men. A very small kitchen was off of the women's room. There was no bathroom. Mr. Li was shown into the men's sitting room. It had a bare cement floor with narrow mattresses placed around the walls. Small cushions marked the spots between the seats. Mr. Li and Ramadan sat and visited.

One by one, Ramadan's little sisters and brothers came into the room. They were shy and tried to push each other into the room. They stared at Mr. Li's eyes and made a joke about being Chinese. Ramadan scolded them, and they soon sat, but their eyes never left Mr. Li's.

Although he felt uncomfortable, Mr. Li tried to ignore the children and look around him. The room was bare, except for a small shelf high in one corner of the room. It held two books, one of them obviously a Qur'an. In another corner, several blankets were stacked on top of each other. After a few minutes, a woman's voice called out, and Ramadan left the room. He returned a few minutes later with a small platter containing four teacups and a brass teapot, plus some leaves. Setting the platter on the floor, he proceeded to place some green leaves in each of the four cups. He then opened the lid of the teapot and poked inside with a small spoon. Then he closed the teapot and began to pour the hot, sweet, thick tea into each of the cups. When he was finished, he passed the first cup to Mr. Li, who took it into his hand. Realizing that it was very hot, he quickly set the cup down on the cement floor. Ramadan passed the other two cups to his three little sisters and two brothers to share.

After a few minutes, Mr. Li tried his tea. It was still very hot, sweet, and had a mint flavor. It was very good. Ramadan and Mr. Li sat for a long time talking and sometimes just looking out the open door at the fields. After what seemed like hours, Ramadan's father came home. Mr. Li realized that this was Friday, and Ramadan's father had probably been attending Friday prayers at the mosque.

Ramadan's father was very friendly and seemed pleased to have Mr. Li in his home. He seemed to ignore Ramadan and concentrated on visiting with Mr. Li. They talked of China, agriculture, livestock, and politics. After a long period, the women called from the other room. Ramadan and his father rose and went to the door where a large tray of food was passed into the room. Ramadan's brothers and sisters disappeared and only the three men moved around the large platter of rice and meat. It was enough to feed ten people. Mr. Li did his best to eat the food, using his hands in the proper manner. He was pleased by the sense that he was adapting to the culture.

After the meal, they visited again for a while and then walked in the fields. Ramadan's father pointed out several plants and talked to Mr. Li about the wheat and barley that they were growing. As the sun started to set, Ramadan and Mr. Li returned to the village where they waited for an hour before a bus came by that had room for them. It was quite late when Mr. Li finally arrived home, but Mr. Li was happy. It had been a good day.

Two days later, Ramadan came by Mr. Li's house. It was late afternoon, and Mr. Li had just finished his afternoon rounds through the hospital. Ramadan seemed happy to see him and asked him about his visit and what he enjoyed the most. Then Ramadan turned to Mr. Li.

"Can you help me with something?"

"Sure, I will try."

"I would like some whiskey. Do you have some?"

Mr. Li was very surprised.

"If you do not have some, could you buy some for me tomorrow? There is a Christian store near here that sells it."

"Why don't you buy your own whisky?" Mr. Li asked.

"Because it is forbidden to Muslims."

"Then why do you want it?"

Ramadan paused. "I want to convert to Christianity. Then I can drink whiskey freely."

Mr. Li was so shocked he didn't know what to say. "You must have some whiskey here. Or beer. You are a Christian, aren't you?"

"Yes, I am a Christian," Mr. Li said slowly. "I don't understand this."

"I want to convert to Christianity," Ramadan said. "I want to travel to China and marry a Christian woman."

"Why?"

"Because being a Christian is better than being a Muslim. You have freedom. I want to drink. I want to enjoy women." He paused. "Do you have any magazines?"

"Magazines? What do you mean?"

"You know—magazines—pictures of women. You are a Christian; you must have some."

"No, I do not have anything like this," Mr. Li said emphatically.

"Can you get me a girl?" Ramadan asked. "I've heard that there are Christian girls that are available. Can you tell me where they are?"

Mr. Li began to get angry. "I know nothing about this," he said, trying to control the anger in his voice.

"I have to go," Ramadan suddenly announced, rising to his feet. "Thank you for the tea." He quickly went to the door and left. Mr. Li sat in shock. What had happened? He wasn't sure what to think.

When Mr. Li met with David again in the hospital courtyard, Mr. Li shared his struggles with Friendship Evangelism. "It's not going too well," he said. "I can make friends, but there really isn't much evangelism. What would happen if I had to leave soon? What would I have accomplished? Making some good friends?" He looked over at David. "How is it going with you? Have you shared about Jesus with any of your friends?"

David hung his head. "No, I've got some good friends, but we seldom talk about religion. They are not really interested in talking about God. They usually talk about sports or politics."

"Perhaps Friendship Evangelism doesn't really work here," Mr. Li suggested. "I wonder if there is another approach."

"Well, you cannot stand on the street corner and preach. And if you talk to people about Jesus, you might get in trouble and get thrown out of the country."

"What do you think we should do?"

"Well," said David with a slight smile. "What would Jesus do?"

"He preached to crowds," Mr. Li thought out loud.

"Did he?" David asked. "He didn't preach. He usually told stories."

"Yes, he told parables."

David looked amazed. "And he didn't explain them, did he?"

"No, people came afterwards, at night sometimes, and asked him what the stories meant."

"I think we should study the Bible," David suggested. "Let's see what the Bible says about different ways to share the gospel with people."

"Okay," said Mr. Li. "Let's meet back here on Thursday and discuss what we found."

The following Thursday, the two met and started to compare notes. They had found a number of different ways of sharing the gospel.

"The first one I found was in I Thessalonians 1:5," David started. "It is one of my favorite verses. The gospel didn't just come in word only. The last part says 'as you know what manner of men we were among you.' Their lives spoke the gospel. So I think the first one should be called Lifestyle Evangelism.' Our lives speak out the truth."

"But," Mr. Li countered, "it wasn't just their lives. The gospel came by word. That was preaching. I was thinking about Jesus. He was always preaching. People called him 'rabbi,' or teacher. Everywhere he went, people respected him because he was seen as a teacher. I think this should be called Teacher-Based Evangelism.'"

"Yes, I see your point," David said. "He did teach, but Peter and Paul stood up and proclaimed the gospel. They weren't just teaching, they were proclaiming it to crowds, or in front of government people. Perhaps we could call that Proclamation Evangelism."

"I think there is another kind," Mr. Li pointed out. "The Bible tells us in Acts 18 that Paul reasoned with the Jews."

"I think that means that he debated with them."

"I think this was not teaching, or proclamation. He was confronting them and their ideas."

"Yes," David said excitedly. "We could call this Confrontation Evangelism."

"Well," Mr. Li said slowly. "What about Friendship Evangelism? Is it in the Bible?"

"I was thinking about that, and the only verse I found that might work was I Thessalonians 2:8: 'we loved you so much that we were delighted to share with you not only the gospel of God but our lives as well, because you had become so dear to us.'"

After they had discussed some more, the two of them took a piece of paper and drew a chart with the five types of evangelism on it:

Lifestyle - Friendship - Teacher-based - Proclamation – Confrontation

David looked at the list. "I think that the order they are in is significant," he commented. "Lifestyle uses the least amount of words. Then friendship."

"Yes, and on the other end, confrontation is the strongest, and then proclamation is next."

"I think it is interesting that teacher-based evangelism is in the middle. I would like to learn more about it," David thought out loud.

"Perhaps we should study this more and meet on Monday to see what we have discovered," Mr. Li suggested as they were getting up to leave. Both of them were excited about what they were learning.

That night, Mr. Li renewed his commitment to the Lord. He asked God for forgiveness because he had been letting his spiritual life slide. He asked God for another opportunity to speak to Ahmed about Jesus.

4

Mr. Li spent a lot of time during the day thinking about what he and David were discovering from the Bible. The idea of different types of evangelism interested Mr. Li very much. One evening, when reading the Bible, Mr. Li read the story of the farmer sowing his seed in Matthew 13. As he thought about the story, Mr. Li suddenly realized that not only were there different types of evangelism, there were different types of people. The Bible referred to people as soil.

"I wonder," Mr. Li said to himself, "if some types of evangelism work better for some types of people?" He thought of the men that he worked with. Most of them were not at all interested in what he had to share. Ahmed, however, was somewhat interested, and sometimes asked him questions. Ahmed was different from the others. He still wasn't seeking the Lord, but he was at least open.

Mr. Li tried to concentrate on his thoughts. Did Jesus ever minister to people who were not interested? He thought about the crowds of people who came for healing, or to see something spectacular. Did they want to hear the message or were they simply coming to see or experience something? Perhaps they were not really interested in what Jesus had to say. How did Jesus reach out to them? He decided that he would ask David the next time they met.

David was also doing some thinking about Jesus, and how he witnessed to others. He could only find one or two places in the Bible where Jesus gave the 'gospel' to people. Usually he told stories. Sometimes he preached. Sometimes he taught people.

Several days later, David and Mr. Li had the opportunity to meet again in the hospital courtyard. They sat under a tree and discussed their findings.

"So there are not only different kinds of evangelism," Mr. Li said, "there are different kinds of audiences. Jesus called them different kinds of soil. Some people are ready to hear, some will hear a little, and some will hear nothing."

David studied the passage in the Bible for a minute. "The farmer scatters seed on all the types of ground," he commented. "He doesn't just go for the good soil. That's what I would do."

"Yes, but how do you tell the good soil from the bad soil?"

"I don't know." David looked puzzled.

"Remember Ramadan," Mr. Li said. "I thought he was going to be a good friend, and someone I could share Christ with, but he was only interested in whiskey and women. He wasn't very good soil."

"But Jesus shared with everyone."

"I don't know," said Mr. Li. "In Matthew 13:26 a few came to Jesus to ask what the stories meant."

"That's it," David said excitedly. "Jesus told stories to the crowds. That's how he spread the seed. Everyone heard the story. No one was offended by the stories. Stories are for everyone. But those who were interested, those who were the good soil, they came back for more."

"Yes," said Mr. Li slowly. "I can see that. But what are we to do, tell stories?"

"But isn't that what Jesus did all the time? If he told stories, shouldn't we?"

Mr. Li looked puzzled. "But I don't know any stories—unless they are Bible stories."

"Maybe those will do."

A couple of days later the Lord provided an opportunity for Mr. Li to share a story. The men had gathered for a tea break. It was hot, and no one was very interested in going back to work very soon. Several of the men were telling stories about things they had done over the weekend. Finally, one of them turned to Mr. Li. "What about you?" he asked. "What did you do this weekend?"

"He probably read his Bible," one of the other men teased.

"Yes," Mr. Li said, recognizing an opportunity. "I read an interesting story that the prophet Jesus told. Would you like to hear it?" He didn't wait long, but started his story right away before anyone could object. "Jesus said that the kingdom of God was like a man who was deeply in debt to his employer. When his employer called him in to repay his debt, he didn't have the money, so he begged his employer to give him time..." As Mr. Li told the story, he sensed that the men were interested. When he finished, he never explained the story. He simply told them, "that's what I read over the weekend."

He poured himself another cup of tea, and one of the other men started talking about sports. After a few minutes, they finished their break and headed out to work. Mr. Li wondered if the story had done any good. "*At least,*" he thought to himself, "*they heard something from the Bible and didn't object.*"

Several days later he had the opportunity to tell another story. Then a few days later Ahmed was feeling sick and asked for the day off. Mr. Li stopped by his room to check on him and then offered to pray for him. To his surprise, Ahmed didn't object at all. Mr. Li bowed his head, thanked God for Ahmed and the work he did every day, and then prayed for his health, asking that God would help his body to heal quickly. That evening Ahmed was feeling better; he seemed to be much warmer towards Mr. Li.

Over the next few months, David and Mr. Li continued to share stories with those around them. Rather than explain them, they would simply tell the stories, and leave the meaning up to the listeners. Sometimes they would say things that would make their listeners think. Sometimes they would offer to pray for people or situations. No one ever refused them when they offered to pray.

One day David told Mr. Li that he was starting to have some good conversations with his landlord's son, Mahmoud. They were discussing some of the Muslims' objections to Christian doctrine. Every time Mahmoud came up with a new objection, David would tell him that they would discuss it the next time they met. Then he would contact Mr. Li and together they discussed what David should say.

David confessed to Mr. Li that he was struggling to explain things in the local language. "You are really much better at the language," David said. "Why don't you meet with Mahmoud and share with him?"

"He is your friend, and you have a relationship with him," Mr. Li answered. "I don't know him at all."

"Well, if it is possible, can I ask him if we could all meet together sometime."

"Okay," Mr. Li said, "but don't force the issue. You want Mahmoud to be comfortable with you. He might be upset if others knew he was asking questions."

Several days later David excitedly reported to Mr. Li: "I've arranged that you visit Mahmoud. He is very excited about meeting you," he added, happily.

"What did you tell him about me?" Mr. Li asked, suddenly alarmed.

"I told him that you spoke the language much better than I do, and that you were a religious teacher who could explain what it was to be a Christian."

Mr. Li was shocked and angry with David. How could he have done such a thing? His language was not very good, and he wasn't a religious teacher. He just wanted to share Jesus with Muslims.

That night, as Mr. Li prayed, he poured out his heart to God. "Oh God," he cried, "how can I do this? I am not a religious teacher. I don't know what to say!"

Suddenly, Mr. Li felt God's presence in the room. It was warm and reassuring. Then he remembered something that the elders of his church had said as they sent him out: "we send you to preach and teach among the Muslim people."

"You really are a teacher," God whispered into his heart. "I have prepared you. You are my instrument."

Mr. Li wrestled with God for a long time until he finally surrendered and felt peace in his heart. Then he asked God to guide him, and he began to write notes on a piece of paper. He would start in the book of Genesis and explain how man was created, and how sin entered the world.

The following day, Mr. Li traveled across town to David's apartment. It was much nicer than the room that Mr. Li had at the worker's compound. David's sitting room had very nice sofa chairs, a bookshelf full of books, a small TV, and a stereo. There were photos of his family on the wall.

David was excited to have Mr. Li finally visit his apartment. He served Mr. Li some tea and sat to discuss their meeting with Mahmoud. Mr. Li shared what God had put in his heart.

After a short time of prayer, there was a knock on the door. It was Mahmoud. Mr. Li glanced over at David. He was dressed in ragged shorts and a T-shirt. Mr. Li had dressed carefully for the occasion and was wearing his best clothes.

Mahmoud was a slender young man with black hair and a small black mustache. He was nicely dressed and smiled when Mr. Li greeted him. He seemed a little surprised that Mr. Li was Asian, not American. "Are you from America?" he asked.

"No," Mr. Li smiled. "I am from China."

"Are you a Christian?" Mahmoud looked puzzled. "I didn't know there were any Christians in China."

"Yes, I am a Christian," Mr. Li responded. "There are many Christians in China, although not everyone is favorable to us."

"I thought that Chinese were infidels, worshiping other gods."

"China has many different kinds of people. Some are atheists and don't believe in any God. But there are millions and millions of Christian believers in China."

"Was it always like this?" Mahmoud asked.

"No, at one time there were few Christians in China. But God has blessed his people, and now we are many." Mr. Li paused. "Would you like to know more about what Christians believe?"

"Yes," Mahmoud smiled. "I used to think that Christians worshiped three gods, but David tells me that you worship only one God."

"Perhaps it would be good if we studied the scriptures themselves to see what they teach us," Mr. Li started. "The truth is in God's word, and we should read it to understand what he is saying to us. This is his word, revealed by the ancient writers and prophets."

"Has it been changed or corrupted?"

"No," Mr. Li explained. "Historians have discovered very ancient copies of these writings, and they have not been changed. Scribes were trained, and they carefully copied the scriptures. Each passage was checked and re-checked by other scribes to make sure that there were no changes."

Mr. Li reached into his bag and got out his Bible and his notepad. "Let's turn to the first chapter and see what it has to say."

David suddenly straightened. "I have a copy here somewhere," he said. "He looked around the room, and then got down on his hands and knees to look under the sofa. "Oh, here it is. I guess it fell on the floor," he said, retrieving the book from under the chair. Mahmoud looked surprised and a bit alarmed.

"Please read the first two verses," Mr. Li began.

Mahmoud took the Bible and quickly read the verses.

"Okay," said Mr. Li. "What do these verses tell us?"

Mahmoud looked blank.

"What do they say?"

Mahmoud was still puzzled.

"Perhaps you should read them again."

Mahmoud again quickly read the verses.

"Okay, what do you think these verses are telling us?"

"What do you mean?" Mahmoud said. "They are from a holy book. I cannot discuss or question them. They mean whatever they say."

Mr. Li smiled. This was indeed very strange. "Mahmoud, do you think God gave us his words to simply memorize and recite, or do you think he wanted us to learn something from them?"

"I suppose he wanted us to learn from them."

"Then perhaps we should discuss what he wanted us to know."

"But isn't it wrong to discuss holy books? I might understand it wrongly. That's why it is important for a teacher to guide me."

"Mahmoud, do you think God is incapable of speaking clearly and plainly?"

"No, he can do anything. But our holy book is very difficult to understand."

"Long ago," Mr. Li began, "the prophet Moses wrote down what God revealed to him about the creation of the world. This knowledge was written so that we might have a record and understand. It is not secret knowledge. It is plain and easy to understand." He paused. "Now let's consider the first verses of the Bible. What does the Bible tell us that God did?"

"He created the world," Mahmoud answered.

"Very good," Mr. Li answered. "Let's discover how he created and what he did."

The three men gathered around the Bible, and together they read the story of creation and discussed it. Mr. Li used the notes that he had prepared the night before to guide Mahmoud through the first two chapters of Genesis. Mr. Li had planned to cover Genesis chapter three, but Mahmoud was having trouble with something that Mr. Li had said.

"From what you are telling me," he said, "the world was a perfect place. Adam and Eve were very happy. Nothing was wrong. Didn't they ever fight?"

"No," Mr. Li smiled. "God is perfect, and what he created was perfect."

"That makes sense," Mahmoud replied, "but the world today is not perfect. Didn't God create this world? Why is the description in the Bible so different from what the world is today?"

"That," said Mr. Li, "is what we will study next." He looked at his watch. "Our time is past, so let's start there on our next study. When can we meet again?" Together they decided to meet in three days' time.

Mr. Li was excited when he returned to his room. Over the next two days, he carefully prepared his notes so that he would be fully ready to guide Mahmoud through Genesis chapter three, and beyond.

The next Bible study went well. When they were finished, Mahmoud asked Mr. Li if he could have a copy of his notes. Mr. Li was surprised. He had prepared his notes for his own use, and he hadn't thought that he would give them away to anyone, especially Mahmoud. But he didn't want to disappoint Mahmoud, so he gave him his notes.

They agreed to meet the following Friday. Mr. Li arrived at David's apartment early, and they talked and prayed together. Then they waited for Mahmoud to arrive. After a while, it appeared that he would be late. They talked some more and waited. After two hours, it was apparent that he wasn't going to show up. As they were leaving, David met his landlord in front of their building. "Is Mahmoud around?" he asked casually after they had greeted one another.

"No, he went out early this morning. I don't know where he went. I don't think he had anything special up. Perhaps he is down in the market with his friends."

David and Mr. Li exchanged glances as they left.

Mr. Li returned home wondering if things were okay. Perhaps Mahmoud was upset with him for something he had said. He waited a few days and then contacted David: "so have you seen Mahmoud?"

"Yes, I talked with him, but he doesn't seem very interested in Bible studies."

"What?" Mr. Li said. "I thought he was doing very well."

"I asked him what the trouble was," David continued. "He seemed to say that the Bible was a very thick book, and we had only studied the first three chapters. He said that it would take years to study our way through it."

"That's too bad." Mr. Li said thoughtfully. "I wasn't planning on taking years. I just wanted to make a good start. There is so much in Genesis that he needs to understand first."

"I asked him if he wanted to do at least one more study, but he declined. When I pushed him a bit, he said that he had your notes, and he would read those."

Mr. Li was very disappointed. He returned home and tried to think through what he could have done better. Perhaps they should have set a limit to the studies. Perhaps he should have told Mahmoud that he could explain the gospel to him in three or four visits, or five or six hours. Perhaps he should not have used notes. It would have been much better if Mahmoud had a Bible rather than his poorly written notes. "Oh, God," he prayed, "I wish I could have done better. Please give me another opportunity to share the gospel and help me do a better job next time."

5

After his experience trying to teach Mahmoud, Mr. Li became discouraged. He had failed in every attempt he had made to share the gospel. So far, he had been in a Muslim country for almost two years. He had learned to speak some of the language, but he had never once been successful in explaining the gospel, and no one had come to Christ. Every time he tried to share the gospel, he either made a mess of it himself, or his listeners became angry with him. Now all he seemed able to do was tell occasional stories from the Bible to the men he was responsible for.

One day, as he was sitting in front of the hospital, watching the crowds of people flowing in and out of the building, bitterness swelled up inside of him. "Look," he said angrily to God. "Look at all of these people. They are all going to hell. And I am here, and I can do nothing. I have given almost two years and—nothing." Mr. Li clenched his teeth. "Oh God, I feel so useless. Why did you bring me here? I've done nothing for you."

In the back of Mr. Li's mind, a plan was slowly forming. He would leave his job and return to China. But first he must find a place in China away from his family and friends, where he would not be known. Perhaps if he moved to some remote area of China he could win people to Christ, plant churches, and thus redeem himself before his family and friends. Here, in this Muslim land, he had only been a failure.

Over the next few days the plan grew in Mr. Li's mind. He calculated when his pay would arrive, how much he had been able to save, and how much an airplane ticket would cost. At the same time, he felt guilty, and wondered if he might be running away from God.

One night he prayed, "God, if you want me to stay in this country, then show me that you are using me. Otherwise, I am going to buy the plane ticket and leave."

That evening he went for a talk in a sparse grove of trees outside the hospital. It was cool in the shade and some of the hospital workers would gather there. Choosing a corner to himself, he stood with his back to the grove and looked out over a nearby valley. He really didn't feel like mixing with others. Then he heard someone approaching him and smelled the person's cigarette smoke.

"Excuse me," a feminine voice spoke, "can I talk with you for a minute?"

He turned and looked with surprise into the face of a young Muslim woman. She was smoking nervously. "I didn't mean to bother you," she started, "but I have a question for you."

"It's okay," he said gently, glad that they were in a common area with other people around. No one seemed to notice them at all.

"I would like to ask you a question about a story you told some time ago."

"Oh?" said Mr. Li. He couldn't remember ever telling a story when this young woman was around.

"Yes, you told the story to my uncle. He told us the story that night. I'm not sure I understood it right. It seemed to be a rather odd story."

"What story is that?"

"It was a story about the prophet Isa," she offered, using Jesus' Arabic name. She paused to draw heavily on her cigarette. "You said that a woman was brought to him that had been caught in adultery."

Mr. Li smiled to himself. He remembered how hard he had worked to make sure he had the right word for adultery, and how hard it had been to remember it when telling the story.

"My uncle told us that Jesus said, 'let he who is without sin cast the first stone.' Is that right?"

"Yes," Mr. Li replied. The girl's eyes were bright and questioning. "But there was more. He told her that her sins were forgiven her, and that she should go and sin no more."

"That's that part I don't understand," she whispered. "How could he forgive sins?" She paused. "Who can forgive sins?" A tear formed in her eye. "If he could forgive her sins, can he forgive mine?"

Suddenly, all the anger and sadness left Mr. Li's heart. He realized that God was answering his prayers. Through this woman, God was telling him that he was being used. This woman was like Nicodemus, who came by night to learn more.

"Yes," he assured the woman, "Jesus can forgive you of your sins, but this is not the place to talk. Can I arrange so you can meet a woman and talk to her?"

The woman's eyes flashed with understanding. "Of course," she said, suddenly aware that they were in a public place.

Mr. Li smiled. "Can I meet you here tomorrow at the same time and arrange with you who you can meet?" She nodded, and then silently left. Mr. Li was very pleased and headed for a telephone where he could call David and ask him to help him find a Christian woman who could help them.

Mr. Li was very happy to learn that David knew of a female Christian missionary named Anna who could help him. They arranged to meet by the grove of trees around dusk. Mr. Li went early to pray. There were very few people around. Once the sun started to set, people would come to the trees in the cool of the evening. For an hour or two, there would be people around, enjoying the breeze that blew in from the valley below. As he prayed, he thanked God that he was again part of what God was doing in someone's life.

After a few minutes, he saw the young woman approaching. Mr. Li looked around in panic. He really didn't want to be seen talking very long to a woman in this place. True, it was a public place, but men and women did not mix freely in this society, and besides that, people might want to know how they knew each other. Before he could think of what to do, she approached him.

She glanced around, realizing that several people were watching. "Excuse me, do you have a light?" she asked, producing her carton of cigarettes.

Mr. Li looked helpless. "I'm sorry; I don't."

She smiled in mock disappointment and produced a lighter from her purse and proceeded to light her own cigarette. "Do you remember me from last night?" she asked quietly.

"Of course," Mr. Li replied. "That's why I returned tonight. I have a friend coming that you can talk to." He paused. "My name is Li," he said. "Mr. Li. I work in the hospital."

"I know," she smiled. "I know all about you. You're the storyteller. I've heard your stories from many people." She brought the cigarette to her lips. "My name is Mona, and I would love to hear one of your stories."

Mr. Li caught a glimpse of David and a young woman coming up the path towards the trees. He sighed in relief. After they had introduced themselves to each other, David suggested that Anna, a western girl, and Mona could stay and talk. He and Mr. Li would leave.

"But first I want to hear a story," Mona said. "I've never heard Mr. Li tell a story."

David shrugged and pointed to Mr. Li. "Okay, let's hear a story."

Mr. Li nodded. He had been praying hard. Then he suggested that they sit on some large rocks. When they were seated, he began:

There once was a young man who enjoyed life and wanted to experience everything. He felt that his home life was far too restricted, and he wanted to get out and go places and do things. So he went to his father to get some money. However, he knew his father wouldn't give him very much, maybe just pocket money, so he asked his father for his inheritance, so he could go out into the world and make his own living. His father was quite surprised and disappointed, but in the end, he gave him his money and the young man set out.

Over the following months, the young man had a good time partying, eating and drinking, and spending his money. With his money he could buy whatever he wanted. Wine, women, song, everything was his—until his money was gone. And when his money left, so did his friends. With no money, he couldn't afford a place to live, and couldn't buy food. Soon, he was homeless and hungry. To make matters worse, there was economic trouble at that time, and life was hard for everyone. With no work, and no money, he began to wander around looking for a way to live.

Mr. Li continued: "finally, he met a man who told him that if he wanted to eat, he could look after his pigs." At this, Mona screwed up her face in disgust. "So he went into the field to watch over the pigs. The problem was the man would only pay him after he worked. The young man was so hungry that he looked through the garbage the pigs were eating to find something to eat." Now Mona looked sick. "Finally, he came to his senses and thought to himself, 'there is plenty to eat in my father's house. Why don't I go back there? I know I have shamed him, but perhaps he will let me work like one of his hired men.' So he headed back."

"I know how this story will end," Mona said sadly. "His family will kill him. When they know how badly he has shamed their name, they will all kill him."

Mr. Li waited for a minute and then continued: "As he came along the road towards his village, his father was sitting out in front of the house. As he watched the road, he recognized his son. With a shout, he leapt to his feet and started running down the road towards his son."

"Here it comes," shuddered Mona.

Mr. Li regarded her a moment, and then continued again, "'My son, my son,' he cried, and he threw his arms around his son. But the son pushed him off. 'Father, I have sinned,' the son said. 'I am unworthy to be your son. Please let me come back as your hired man. I am so cold and hungry.' His father shouted for the people in the house to come."

"I knew it. This is going to have a terrible ending."

Mr. Li smiled and shook his head. "Not this time," he said softly. "The young man's father called for the family robe to be brought and with it he covered up his son's rags. Then he called for shoes to be put onto his feet. Last, he took the family ring from off his own hand and put it onto his son's finger. He then called for everyone to prepare a great feast, for his long-lost son was home."

Mr. Li turned to Mona. "Jesus told this story to show us that God is not like a great Sultan, but rather like a loving father."

There was a long pause, and then Mona whispered under her breath, "a thing never once seen before: a flying turtle." Mr. Li recognized this as a local proverb. For a moment there was silence, then Mona spoke again in a very soft voice, "I would like to know more about this. It is so different from everything I've been taught."

After some sharing, Mr. Li and David walked back towards the hospital. Anna and Mona exchanged phone numbers and arranged to meet the next day. Mr. Li's heart was rejoicing as he returned to his small room. Perhaps, just perhaps, God was going to do something through him. In his heart, he knew that he would not return to China. God wanted him just where he was.

6

Mr. Li arrived at Zay'id's home exactly at 8:00, as he was told when he was invited. He was welcomed and shown into the formal reception room where Zay'id father was waiting. Zay'id shook his hand and warmly welcomed him. He smiled happily and was pleased that Mr. Li had come to his home. Zay'id was an employee at the hospital, and he had heard some of the stories that Mr. Li had told. He had invited Mr. Li to visit him and was now evidently pleased that he had arrived.

As they sat and talked, Zay'id rose and took a coffee urn and two very small cups. Carefully he poured a very small amount into a cup and passed it to Mr. Li, who looked into the cup. There was only about 1/3 of a cup full in the bottom of his cup. He wondered why he had not been offered a full cup. Zay'id's father drank his cup, and before he returned it to Zay'id, he rolled the cup back and forth several times. Mr. Li noticed it. Zay'id laughed.

"This is new for you, isn't it?" Zay'id asked. Mr. Li nodded.

"Well, when you don't want any more coffee, you shake your hand back and forth to indicate that you have had enough."

Mr. Li sipped it. He rolled his hand several times, and Zay'id took his cup. Then they sat and visited.

Zay'id's father soon started telling him about their local culture. "There once was a western man who learned about our culture. He learned to shake his cup when he didn't want any more to drink. Then when he was eating the meal, his host kept insisting that he eat more, so he finally took the great tray of food and shook it back and forth." Zay'id and his father laughed loudly. Mr. Li smiled and tried to join in.

Soon Zay'id poured out several glasses of sweet tea, and they sat talking and visiting. Then, after an hour into their visit, Zay'id rose and took the coffee urn. He carefully poured 1/3 of a cup into each one and served Mr. Li and then his father. After the very small cup of coffee, they continued their visiting. Mr. Li wondered about the small cups of coffee. He wondered if this was some sort of ceremony.

When they were drinking tea and eating some simple food, he asked Zay'id about the coffee. Zay'id smiled. "I'm sorry. I guess you don't understand our culture. When you visit a home, you are offered coffee three times. The first 1/3 cup means 'peace.' This cup of peace is offered soon after you enter the house. If it is not offered, then we really don't want you here." He looked stern. "Maybe we would kill you." Then he smiled to indicate he was joking. Mr. Li wasn't quite sure.

"I'm glad I was offered the cup of peace," Mr. Li joked.

"Then halfway through the visit, we offer the cup of friendship. This indicates that we are more than just at peace with each other. We are friends."

"And you offered me the cup of friendship. That is very nice. I hope we will always be good friends," Mr. Li added. Then he paused. "What does the last cup mean?"

"That one you haven't had yet. You get that at the end of the visit. That is the cup of the sword."

Mr. Li was shocked. "The sword?" he asked. "I hope you never offer me the cup of the sword."

"Why, are you afraid?" Zay'id teased. "It is because you do not understand it. What the cup of the sword means is that we will protect you with our lives. We will use our swords to protect you from whoever you are afraid of. No questions asked. We are bound by honor to protect you, and you are bound by honor to protect us. That is how deep our friendship goes."

Mr. Li sighed in relief. After another hour of visiting, he looked at his watch. "I'm sorry," he said, "but if I am to find a bus back to the hospital, I need to go soon."

"Not before you drink the 'cup of the sword,'" Zay'id smiled, offering him another 1/3 of a small cup of coffee. Mr. Li graciously accepted before leaving.

Several weeks had passed since Mr. Li had last seen David, who was away at a conference. Mr. Li looked forward to having his young American friend around so they could encourage one another and learn from one another. When David returned, he was very excited. He had been to a neighboring country where he had attended a conference for Christian workers reaching Muslims. At this conference, they had taught him all about contextualization, or how to put the Christian message into a Muslim context. They had taught that since the word 'Islam' means to be submitted to God, Christians could say that they were Muslims.

David was now excited to be a *Muslim for Christ*. At the conference they had taught him how to face Mecca when he prayed and how to act like a Muslim. David felt that this would help remove tensions between him and other Muslims. After all, they would see him as one of their own, and would accept him better. During his visit with Mr. Li, he announced that he was going to go to the mosque and pray.

"David," Mr. Li protested, "You are an American. If you go to the mosque, there may be fanatics there that will oppose you!"

"No, I'll be okay. I've got an invitation to go to the mosque from the Muslim guard at my apartment building. I asked him if I could and he got me the invitation."

"David, what do you want to do there?" Mr. Li asked in alarm.

"I can go stand there and pray with them, just like they do. I can tell them that I am a Muslim for Christ."

"David, I think I should go with you. I'm afraid that something will happen to you. Maybe I can act as your translator. You speak English to them and I will translate. Don't use any Arabic. That way, I can be in between. Perhaps they will be more merciful to me, as I am not an American."

"Okay," he agreed, "but we need to go soon if we are to get to the mosque near to my house."

When they arrived, there were about twenty men at the mosque. A young man came to greet them and welcome them at the door.

"Hello. My name is Mr. Li and I am a translator for this man. I didn't come for religious reasons, just to translate." He smiled, and they were off to a good start. But it didn't last long. They had some tough questions for David.

"So you think you are Muslim?" someone asked.

"Alhamdulila," David responded, which means 'Praise be to God.'

"What about your Islamic religion? what do you think?" another persisted.

Mr. Li did not envy David that night. He was squeezed and squeezed. Slowly they backed him into corners. At one point Mr. Li whispered, "David, let's go."

But they kept pressing him: "Do you believe that the Qur'an is the Word of God?"

"There are many good things in the Qur'an," he answered, with Mr. Li's translation.

"No, wait. That is not what we asked. Do you believe that the whole Qur'an was spoken by God himself?"

Then someone else interrupted them in English. "Hold on here; you don't need interpretation. I can speak better English than your translator." Mr. Li recognized that the man had a good American accent. Perhaps he was a professor at a university. Mr. Li felt really humbled by his English.

"Tell me, Mr. David," the man continued in English, "what does Islam mean to you? Is it running to the light of Islam from the darkness of Christianity?"

"*Oh my goodness,*" Mr. Li thought, "*this is very direct.*"

"Well, there are many good things in Islam..."

"Let's go back to that question that my colleague just asked you. Did you say that you believe in the Qur'an as a whole?" He spoke like a lawyer.

"*Okay, David, enjoy it,*" Mr. Li thought to himself. "*You wanted this; let's see if you can get out of it.*"

Then, to his horror, David said, "Yes."

"Excuse me, please." Mr. Li interrupted. "Can I halt this talk? Let's get out of here, David."

One of the other men suddenly spoke up. During the discussion, he had been looking at Mr. Li and not saying anything. He just stared. When Mr. Li told David to stop, he said, "excuse me. Can I ask you a question, Mr., ah... what was the name?"

"Mr. Li."

"Mr. Li, are you two evangelists? Are you trying to reach us for Christianity?"

"Yes," Mr. Li admitted, still wanting to run. "Look, I apologize for my friend. He just wanted to share with you his love through an Islamic cloak, but it doesn't work. We are Christians and we are sorry to have offended you."

"Why didn't you just talk to us? Why not come and say, 'We want to tell you about Christ?' Talk plainly. Why do you come here and lie that you are a Muslim?"

"Look, I'm here as a translator," Mr. Li protested.

The man scowled. "You're here as his boss."

"No, I'm not his boss. We both work at different companies."

"You both are evangelists, and you are guiding him. I watched you talking to David in English. You really wanted him to say something different, and you added some things in your interpretation. We all know English here."

"Oh," Mr. Li gasped. "*Who are these people?*" he thought to himself. "Okay," Mr. Li said aloud, "I apologize. I am an evangelist. We just wanted to share about Christ."

"Why didn't you tell us from the beginning? You could have sat here in front, and we would have given you time and listened to you."

"Oh really? I'm sorry. Good night." Mr. Li took David by the arm and together they left the mosque. David was really ashamed of himself.

"Do you really believe in the Qur'an?" Mr. Li asked him later when they were back at the hospital.

"No, no, I just didn't know what to say," David admitted.

Mr. Li and David then got on their knees and asked God to show them a better way to answer questions when they were put to them.

7

Every Tuesday, Mr. Li had the afternoon free, so he would visit the market street in the center of town where Zay'id's father owned a shop. This Tuesday, when he dropped by the store, a young boy sat at the desk. Mr. Li was somewhat disappointed as he wished to buy something from the store. However, since this was the store of his friend's father, we went ahead and ordered what he needed. He sat by the table while the young man went about getting things that Mr. Li had asked for. When he was done, he carefully packed them all in a bag, slowly adding up the price. Mr. Li, who was always very careful with his money, was also doing the math. He had purchased most of the items before, so he knew roughly how much they cost.

When the boy was done, Mr. Li asked him how much it would be. In his head, he had calculated around 20 dinars. The young man thought for a moment and then replied, "forty dinars." Mr. Li's heart sank. Even if they bartered back and forth, they might end up at thirty, which would still be too much money. Frustration began to build in him.

"Can we check the prices of the individual items?" he asked.

The young boy looked doubtful, but he emptied the bag onto the desk. Each item required that he check the notebook that Zay'id's father kept in a drawer. As they were nearing the end of the process, Zay'id's father returned. He greeted Mr. Li warmly and then asked the young boy what was happening. The young boy's face filled with pride.

"I am selling the foreigner these things," he said, indicating the goods on the table.

"And what price did you come up with?"

"I am charging him forty dinars," he said with pride.

Zay'id father looked alarmed. "No, no, you don't understand," he said to the boy. "Forty dinars is the far price. This is Mr. Li, a good friend of my family. We need to charge him the near price."

"Oh," said the boy. "In that case, the price is 20 dinars."

Zay'id father smiled, and Mr. Li happily paid for his goods. Before he could leave, he was invited to drink tea and visit. Then he was invited to their home for the supper meal.

"Please come," Zay'id's father said. "Today is a special meal. Yesterday, my son graduated from secondary school, and today our whole family will celebrate."

Mr. Li had time, so he waited until the store closed and together they made their way to Zay'id's home. There Mr. Li met Wasfi, Zay'id's younger brother, who had just received his school grades. As they waited for the meal, relatives began to arrive. Soon, the sitting room was filled with men, all uncles and cousins of Zay'id and Wasfi.

Just when Mr. Li thought that the room was totally full, there was a commotion, and the center of the room was cleared so that a large platter filled with meat could be brought in. Wasfi took a water jug, a basin and a towel over his arm and began to move from guest to guest so that the men could wash their right hands. The women and younger children were obviously in another room.

After everyone had washed their hands, Zay'id's father motioned for them to gather around and eat. Mr. Li squeezed in beside the other men, and using his right hand, he began to eat from the platter. The other men were pleased at his ability to eat with his fingers, and Mr. Li felt very much united with them all.

After the meal, Wasfi again brought the water jug, basin, and towel, and moved from man to man until everyone has washed his right hand. No sooner had he finished this before glasses of hot sweet tea were passed around the room.

Now that everyone had eaten, and they had tea, there was an opportunity to relax and talk. Mr. Li sensed, however, that there was a purpose to this meeting. Wasfi's grandfather opened the conversation. "So, my son, how were your school grades?"

"Oh father, I passed all my subjects."

"May I see your report?"

"Yes, here it is." Wasfi presented his report, and one by one the men around the room took the piece of paper and examined it. Wasfi seemed nervous. As the paper passed Mr. Li, he could see that Wasfi had done well in some of his subjects, and his average was around 80%.

"Well, what are we going to do with Wasfi?" the grandfather asked.

"His marks are good enough to go to technical school," someone offered.

"I had hoped for a dentist," another man said.

"You always want a dentist," another answered. "It's just your bad teeth."

"Yes, but he needs 90% to get into dental school," the first man replied. "So dental school is out."

"What about the army?" another asked.

"It's an option. He could go for officer's training."

"Let's not forget technical school," another uncle spoke up. "There is a growing need for those who install central plumbing. How many of us will want central plumbing in our homes in the next couple of years?"

"But what about the summertime? What does he do then?"

"Install air conditioning," the uncle responded. "More and more homes are getting air-conditioning."

"So what about it?" the grandfather said as he turned to Wasfi. "What is it that you are thinking about?"

"I'm interested in computers," Wasfi answered. "I'm sure there are lots of jobs for computer operators."

"Yes," another uncle exclaimed. "They are looking for computer operators over at the customs house."

"Customs!" exclaimed another man. "That would be excellent. Our family has no representation in customs."

"Nor any dentists," a familiar voice complained.

"How long will this training take?" someone asked, and the conversation turned to how quickly Wasfi could start training, and if he might still get a job at the customs building.

That evening, the family decided that Wasfi should pursue computer training, and if not, plumbing. His uncles discussed how much each of the family members needed to contribute to pay for his schooling.

The following day, Zay'id dropped by Mr. Li's room after work. As was his custom, he would bring some food from his family, or just stop for a visit. After a while, Zay'id's questions turned to religion, and he began asking Mr. Li significant questions about what Christian's believed. Mr. Li was now spending considerable time praying for Zay'id and his family, and he decided that it was now time to start to share more openly with Zay'id.

The next time Zay'id stopped by, Mr. Li asked him if he would like to learn about Christianity and what Christians believed. He would be happy to take him through a couple of lessons, or to invite a friend of his over, who could explain Christian beliefs to him. Zay'id thought about it for a moment and then declined. However, after several weeks had passed, Mr. Li asked again and Zay'id agreed to the study with him.

After they had met several times for lessons, Mr. Li began to wonder about religious freedom in a Muslim country. It seemed very strange to him. In the three years that he had been this Muslim country, he had never heard of any government reactions to Christianity, and there was no apparent government persecution of Christians. He was not restricted from studying with Zay'id, and a bookstore in town sold Bibles in the local language. He began to wonder if the talk about persecution from Muslims was all lies.

The following week, he asked Zay'id what it might mean if a Muslim changed his faith to become a Christian. How would this affect the Muslim's life? Zay'id thought for a minute and then said that it would probably be very dangerous. He might be killed. This puzzled Mr. Li, as he had never seen any government action against Christians.

One day, an excited cleaner came running down the hall to Mr. Li's room. "Mr. Li," he called out excitedly. "You are needed at the pharmacy. There is a big problem developing there, and the director wants all the heads of departments down there right away, including you."

Mr. Li put on his coat and hurried over to the pharmacy building. A large crowd had gathered outside and angry voices were shouting and arguing. Realizing that the hospital director wanted responsible people near the trouble, Mr. Li began to make his way through the crowd. He eventually stepped up near the hospital director, who was arguing with several men. Mr. Li looked around. There seemed to be a number of very angry men, some of them armed with knives, and a few held pistols.

"How do you know he did it?" the hospital director protested.

"The medicine came from him," one of the men shouted, pointing at the hospital pharmacist. "We checked with other doctors. It is the wrong medicine."

The hospital director looked at the box of pills that the men held up. "You are right. This is not the medicine he should have had."

"And my brother died from that medicine," one angry man shouted. "Because he died, that man will die." He pointed at the pharmacist, who was hiding behind the hospital administrator. Several men behind him were frantically talking on cell phones.

"Calm down everyone, this needs to be handled properly," the hospital administrator protested, waving his hands. "No one is going to kill anyone here. That will solve nothing."

"If you protect him, then we will kill you, too."

Mr. Li wondered if the few hospital employees standing near the administrator would be enough to handle the crowd.

Just then two policemen pushed their way through the crowd. They stood between the hospital people and the angry crowd and demanded to know what was going on. After stopping the shouting, they began to put together the story. The angry crowd believed that the hospital pharmacist had given the wrong medicine to a man, and after he took it, he died. His relatives had gathered, and they had come to the hospital seeking revenge.

"You cannot touch him," the policemen said. "If you cannot solve this, we will take the pharmacist to the police station, and you can state your case there."

"It's blood for blood," an angry man cried out. "This man's life must be taken because of my brother's life."

Just then a group of well-dressed businessmen pushed their way into the crowd. They came up behind the hospital administrator and formed a protective wall around the pharmacist.

"We speak for the pharmacist," one of the men said. "We are his family. Who dare's challenge us?"

The man who lost his brother explained what tribe they were from, and what the problem was. Men on several sides of the argument started calling on their cell phones.

"The honor of our family is at stake" the brother said. "We demand blood for blood."

"Who will speak for your side of the family?" a businessman asked.

"My uncle will be here in a few minutes. He will represent us."

The onlookers in the crowd started to drift away as they waited for the tribal representative to arrive. In the meantime, several more policemen arrived and the two groups were separated on opposite sides of the hospital courtyard. Mr. Li stepped aside and watched the process.

After some time, the two representatives met in the center of the courtyard, each backed by his tribal family. The case was laid out again. Mr. Li noted with interest that the tribal representatives were much respected by each side of the family. Obviously, they were men of renown and respect.

After an hour of debate and argument, the pharmacist's family agreed to pay ten thousand American dollars in cash to the offended family. The men discussed this for a few minutes and then it was agreed. A checkbook was produced, and the money was immediately paid. The policemen stayed until the event was over and the crowd had dissipated.

That night, Mr. Li thought about what had happened. Suddenly, it was very clear to him. Muslims take great pride in being Muslims. If a Muslim leaves Islam, he dishonors his family, and they will want to take revenge. Persecution would come from the immediate family members, not from the government.

As Mr. Li thought about this, he wondered if there might be a way to demonstrate that following Christ was an honorable thing, not a dishonorable thing. Maybe, just maybe, the family wouldn't be so upset.

8

In the months that followed, Zay'id continued to meet with Mr. Li. During their times together, Mr. Li would teach Zay'id from the scriptures. Mr. Li began with the story of creation and then found he needed to explain the prophets to Zay'id.

"All of the prophets did two things," Mr. Li explained. "All of them pointed to sin in the people's lives and called them to repentance. The second thing was, all of the prophets pointed to someone, a promised person, who would come after them. This person was known as the Messiah." Taking his Bible in hand, Mr. Li began to show Zay'id what the Old Testament had to say about the promised Messiah. "All of the prophets looked forward to the one that God would send who would free his people. Not just physically, but free them from the power of sin and evil."

When the time was right, Mr. Li introduced the person of Jesus Christ. Very carefully he took Zay'id through the scriptures, demonstrating that Jesus fulfilled everything that was spoken about him by the prophets. "They even predicted his death, how he would be led as a lamb to the slaughter," Mr. Li pointed out. "This would be God's sacrificial lamb for the sins of the world."

Zay'id carefully studied these things. Not much was said about Islam or the prophet Muhammad. Mr. Li concentrated on Jesus and let Zay'id come to his own conclusions about Muhammad. All of the prophecies pointed to Jesus. After carefully explaining what it meant to be a true follower of Jesus, and the costs that were involved, Mr. Li asked Zay'id if he would like to become a follower of Jesus. To his surprise, Zay'id said "yes." A few minutes later they were on their knees and Zay'id prayed to accept Jesus' death on the cross in place of his sin.

In the weeks that followed, Mr. Li was excited about teaching Zay'id new truths from the scriptures. However, he cautioned Zay'id not to say too much until he had studied more and could give good answers for the things he now believed. After several weeks, Zay'id began to look downcast, so Mr. Li kept the study very short and decided to try and find out what was bothering Zay'id.

"I don't like hiding things from my family," he said. "My family asks me what I am doing here all the time, and why I don't come home straight from work." He paused. "Sometimes I lie to them and tell them that I stopped to watch a movie, or visited the shops in town. I think they are beginning to suspect something."

Mr. Li thought for a moment. "Do you want to stop meeting for a while?"

"I love reading the Bible and learning about Jesus," Zay'id said. "I don't want to stop now. But I also love my family, and I don't want to disappoint them either."

"Perhaps we should meet less often," Mr. Li suggested. "The men here are beginning to wonder about us as well. We are always sitting together, talking."

"Is there some way that I can get a Bible and read it in secret?"

"I will ask around and see if I can get you a small Bible that you can put in your shirt pocket. Perhaps you can read at home, and then our discussions will be shorter."

Zay'id looked discouraged. "Will it always be like this? Will I always need to be careful and live two different lives?"

Mr. Li considered this for a minute. "No," he said. "We are going to start praying about this, and seeing if there isn't a way that you can openly be a follower of Jesus."

Every day or two, Zay'id would meet with Mr. Li for Bible study. On the days between, they would meet for coffee at the hospital cafeteria, or Zay'id would drop in to visit in Mr. Li's room. Mr. Li had cut up a small New Testament so that Zay'id could take one or two pages home each day in his shirt pocket. When time allowed, Zay'id would read the pages, often studying them again and again.

One day Zay'id's mother was washing clothes and asked Zay'id for his shirt. Without thinking, Zay'id passed his shirt to his mother and went to his room for another one. When he returned, he discovered his mother reading the pages from his pocket. Zay'id was horrified—terrified of being discovered. He quickly snatched the pages from his mother. When his mother asked what they were, he said they were "nothing," and left the house.

A short time later a shaken Zay'id related the story to Mr. Li. When he finished, Mr. Li sat and looked at him. Then, quietly, Mr. Li said, "so that's what it is. It's all nothing?" Zay'id was stunned. This was not what he had meant to portray as he told the story. Mr. Li continued: "after all this time together, after everything you've said and done—it's all nothing?"

"No!" Zay'id protested. "It's not 'nothing.' I've met Jesus. He has changed my life. Before this, my life was empty. God was far away. But now He has touched my life—He has changed me and I'm His follower. It's not 'nothing.'"

Mr. Li smiled. "Zay'id, that's wonderful. You've just said your testimony. Do you think you could tell that to your family?" Together they looked into the Word of God, studying what it meant to talk about one's faith and not to be ashamed of the Gospel of Christ.

The next day, Zay'id's oldest brother came to talk to him. He explained that their father had sent him to discover what the papers were that their mother had found. Zay'id paused and gathered his strength knowing that Mr. Li was praying for him. He then shared his testimony with his brother. His brother listened, and then said, "I'll talk it over with our father."

Several days later, Zay'id's oldest brother approached him again. "I've talked it over with father," he said, "and we've agreed that during the last few months we have seen a real change in your life. You really are different, better than before. We've decided to let you continue to read the writings of the prophet Isa."

That night, as Zay'id met with Mr. Li, he was so amazed and filled with joy and thanks. He made his first step in coming out. The road would not be easy, but now that he had started to walk it, he was excited and encouraged. Perhaps someday he could be free to love Jesus openly in his community, and not just by himself, but others with him.

The next day was a holiday for Zay'id. He showed up at Mr. Li's room and he stayed for hours. The following day, as soon as his work was over, he came back. This began to happen day after day. At first, Mr. Li welcomed Zay'id, but he soon found all his time taken up with Zay'id. This began to worry him, and he spoke to David about it.

"Don't stop him," David encouraged Mr. Li. "Let him come to your room. I'm sure he needs a place to go. You don't need to entertain him. Just give him a place where he can read and meditate. He may just enjoy being around you, in a place where there isn't foul language and continual discussion about women and money."

At first, Mr. Li felt awkward as Zay'id would come regularly to his room, often for hours at a time. He would frequently spend an hour or two reading from the Bible, then he would ask questions, and later would read again. Zay'id enjoyed it when David visited Mr. Li's room as well. Sometimes David, or Mr. Li, would sit with him and discuss the scriptures with him. Weeks went by and Mr. Li and David gave Zay'id as much attention as they could, all the while allowing him space to just read the Bible or listen to Christian music.

A few weeks later, Zay'id brought a young man to the Mr. Li's room. He explained to him that this room was available if he wanted to read the Bible, listen to Christian music, or discuss Christian things. In the weeks that followed, the two young men grew into three. They didn't want Mr. Li to do anything except allow them to read, meditate, and ask questions when they had them. To them, the important thing was that they had a place to go to for quiet solitude and fellowship. Mr. Li hadn't quite realized it, but in his little room a church had come into being.

9

The sun was very hot when Mr. Li left the hospital for the shops in the center of town. He was going out to look for a gift to take to Mahmoud, the son of David's landlord. Sometime after Mr. Li's failed attempt to share the gospel with Mahmoud, Mahmoud had received a scholarship to study at a distant university. Now a year had passed and Mahmoud had returned. Mahmoud's father had invited David and Mr. Li to their house to celebrate. Since this was an important occasion, Mr. Li spent the whole afternoon searching for a suitable gift. He considered buying chocolates, but the sun was too hot, and they would melt before he returned to the hospital. He stopped and looked at watches, but he couldn't decide. He looked at fancy pen sets. He stopped at the sweet shop and looked at pastries. Then he looked in a book shop. The books were not very interesting, but Mr. Li's attention was drawn to the calculators. Since Mahmoud was studying math, perhaps a calculator would make a nice gift. After looking at them for a while, Mr. Li realized that they were quite expensive, and Mahmoud would probably already have one. As he walked down the street he continued to ponder his problem. A year earlier, Mahmoud had started Bible studies with them, and he wanted to make a good impression so that the opportunity might come to start them again.

A few minutes later something caught his attention and he smiled. In a shop window was a set of eight small tea glasses with gold colored trim. They looked very nice, and the price was within what he wanted to spend. He asked the shop keeper to wrap them nicely as a gift and then he returned to the pastry shop to buy a box of good quality pastries as a second gift. Then he rushed home to prepare for the party.

Putting on his best clothes, Mr. Li took the bus across town to the apartment block where David lived. His landlord lived on the second floor above the stores, while David lived on the fourth floor. When he turned the corner onto the street, Mr. Li was shocked to discover that the street had been closed, and a very large black woven tent now occupied the street. The tent was filled with white plastic chairs and loudspeakers were blaring very loud music. Mahmoud's father approached him and welcomed him. He shook his hand warmly and then led him over to where Mahmoud was sitting.

Mahmoud stood to his feet and welcomed Mr. Li, who smiled, greeted him, and placed his presents on the small table before Mahmoud where other presents were also sitting. Then Mahmoud's father took Mr. Li around the tent, introducing him to the other men who were present. There were no women in sight. Most of the men were family members, and a few were visiting neighbors. Small cups of bitter coffee were passed around, followed by small glass cups of sweet tea. During the following hour, more and more men arrived. The music was so loud that Mr. Li had to shout to be heard.

Eventually David arrived. He was dressed in shorts and an older t-shirt, with sandals on his feet. He looked shabby compared to the other men present. Mr. Li noticed that he did not bring a present. He spent most of his time with the young teenagers in a back corner and did not go around the tent greeting the men. Mr. Li, for his part, slowly made his way around the tent, greeting different people until he got near to David.

"How are you?" David asked him with a smile. Mr. Li was prepared to shake David's hand, as he had been shaking everyone else's hand, but David never offered his own and seemed to ignore Mr. Li's hand.

"I'm fine," Mr. Li responded, quite disappointed with David's appearance. "I see you came to the party. I'm hoping we can make amends with Mahmoud and rebuild our relationship. It would be nice to start studies with him again."

"Yes, that would be good," said David thoughtfully.

"Did you bring him a gift?" Mr. Li asked gently, not wanting to embarrass David, but wanting to encourage him to think about what he could do to help build the relationship.

"Gift?" David frowned. "No, I didn't think of a gift." He looked surprised. "I guess I should get him something. It looks like others have been bringing gifts." He paused. "Do you think that they noticed that I didn't bring a gift?"

Mr. Li looked at him steadily without answering.

"I guess you noticed," David said glumly. "I'll slip out and get him something."

Mr. Li returned to chatting with people while David rushed off to a nearby store. Mr. Li reminded himself that David was young and an American. Perhaps that was why he was acting so strangely.

After what seemed like a very long time, David returned. His present wasn't wrapped, but it had a ribbon and a bow on it. When he placed it before Mahmoud, Mr. Li realized to his horror that it was a mirror. "*What is David thinking? Is he purposely trying to destroy what is left of our relationship with Mahmoud? Doesn't he know that a mirror gives the message: you need to look at yourself! Improve yourself!*"

Later that evening, Mahmoud's father called everyone to attention, and announced that the food was coming. The men all stood back as great trays of rice and meat were brought into the tent. The men crowded around them and began to eat. David, it seemed, had already left.

After the party, Mr. Li returned home, discouraged and very upset with David. Two weeks went by and he heard nothing from David, nor did David visit the hospital compound. By this time, Mr. Li was very upset with the young American missionary.

The following week, Mr. Li fell ill. First, he had a fever, and then his stomach became sick. He spent three days between his bed and the bathroom. He felt that he was going to die and several times cried out to God for strength. Ahmed dropped by the second evening and brought Dr. Wilson with him, who gave him some medicine. After a few days, he began to feel better. By the end of the week, he was up and around, although he was still not standing for long periods of time.

It was then that David arrived. He came happily through the hospital courtyard, and when he spotted Mr. Li, he smiled. "I've got some good news," he said. "My mission agency has arranged that I can go home to America in three weeks. I'm so excited about going to see my family."

Mr. Li was happy for David, but he was also disturbed. David had not greeted him and had not asked how he was. He showed no interest in Mr. Li and obviously didn't know how sick Mr. Li had been.

"Here, I have something for you," David said. "Some of the other American missionaries and I got some money together to help you, being from China and all. We figured you could use this." He thrust an envelope into Mr. Li's hands. Mr. Li felt very embarrassed. *"Why did David tell the other missionaries that he is poor? What else is he telling them?"*

"I've got to go," David said abruptly, and he turned to leave. As Mr. Li watched him go, he tried to suppress the anger and frustration growing within him. *"Maybe it's good you go back to America,"* he thought to himself, but he didn't dare say it.

Several days later, Dr. Wilson, the Christian doctor at the hospital, sat with Mr. Li for lunch in the hospital cafeteria.

"How are things with you, Mr. Li?" Dr. Wilson asked.

"Oh, I'm feeling much better now. Thank you for your help."

"I'm glad you are better physically, but you look sad, or disturbed about something. Are things okay back in China?"

"Yes, my family is all well."

"How are things here at the hospital?" Dr. Wilson asked.

"Everything is fine here, too. I enjoy my work and it seems to be going well."

"Then what is the problem?"

"It's my American friend, David. I just don't understand him."

Dr. Wilson smiled. "You seem to be adjusting to the Muslims okay, but now you are having cultural problems with Americans?"

"I don't know if it is cultural problems," Mr. Li replied. "Maybe I don't understand him. But he seems to do everything wrong. I wonder if he is angry with me for something."

"What seems to be the problem?" Dr. Wilson asked. Mr. Li then outlined what had happened at the party some weeks before. Dr. Wilson chuckled. "It sounds like David is not very culturally sensitive. I'm sure he doesn't mean what you think he communicated. Perhaps you should talk to him and tell him all the things he was doing wrong."

"They weren't really wrong, they were offensive," Mr. Li explained.

"But if he acted wrongly, then he needs to learn how to act correctly in the future."

Now it was Mr. Li's turn to be puzzled. Didn't Dr. Wilson understand that David had been offensive? This wasn't a question about right and wrong—it was about acting appropriately, about offending others. Dr. Wilson didn't seem to quite understand, either. Perhaps it was because he was an American, too.

10

Several days later, David stopped by the hospital for a visit during the lunch break. He seemed happy and genuinely glad to see Mr. Li. As they talked, Mr. Li wondered if he might be able to direct the conversation towards the party the evening before. He was curious to know why David acted like he did. Thankfully, David broached the topic first.

"Thank you for your help at the party the other day. I totally forgot about bringing a gift. I never remember those kinds of things."

"Really?" asked Mr. Li. "Gifts are important. Don't you like getting gifts?"

"I never really got many gifts when I was growing up," David said. "My parents always bought me whatever I needed when I wanted it. I guess gift giving is important in this culture."

"Is it not important in all cultures?"

"No, I don't think so. The important thing was that I was there. The right thing to do was to show up. I forgot that in this culture, the right thing to do is to also give a gift."

Mr. Li was puzzled. "So you gave a gift because it was the right thing to do?"

"Of course," David answered. "I was wrong to forget a gift." He paused. "When you reminded me, I felt really guilty. It was my bad. So I went and bought him a really nice gift."

"Your gift was a really nice gift?"

"Yes, that mirror cost me a lot of money. Did you see the pattern that was engraved on it? I hope that the nice mirror makes up for my coming without a gift." Mr. Li looked at David for a long time. David looked guilty. "Did I do something else wrong?"

"I don't know. In my country, we would never give a mirror as a gift."

"Really?" David looked puzzled. "Why not? It's a very useful item."

"David," Mr. Li began. "Gifts speak about what is in your heart. A sweet gift speaks of sweetness between you. Dishes, like the teacups, speak of hospitality and warmness. A gift of medicine would express my concern for your well-being. But a mirror…" Mr. Li was lost for words.

David waited impatiently. "Yes, a mirror. What does a mirror speak of?"

"A mirror speaks of examining yourself. It says: you should look at yourself. It is like criticizing."

"That's stupid," David countered. "Gifts don't speak. A gift says, 'I'm a gift.' It says that I did the right thing in bringing one. Gifts don't have meaning. That's simply wrong and stupid. I did the right thing in bringing a gift, not the wrong thing."

Mr. Li was shocked at David's response. "In my country, people would be offended by the gift of a mirror."

"Well, that is your country," David argued. "This is not your country. It is not your culture. Here the right thing to do is to bring a gift. I did the right thing. I don't think that gifts speak."

"In this culture, everything speaks," Mr. Li said softly. "Even the different cups of coffee have different names."

"That's absurd," David responded. "I've never heard that."

"Ask your Muslim friends sometime."

David was about to respond when Zay'id entered the courtyard and greeted them. He offered to buy them tea from the little teashop, and together they sat on some large rocks under the trees.

David began. "I'm so glad I have both of you together. Perhaps you can help me with a language problem."

"Zay'id can help you," Mr. Li smiled. "I'm still a learner."

"I've been trying to share the gospel with a friend, and I need to know the word for 'guilt.' All of us are guilty before God."

Zay'id and Mr. Li exchanged glances. "This one is for you," Mr. Li said with a smile. "I don't know the word for guilt."

"What do you mean by guilt?" Zay'id asked.

"Well, if you did a bad crime, and were taken to jail, then you are guilty."

"Yes, murderers and rapists are guilty," Zay'id replied, "but you cannot use that word with your friend. It is a very strong word, and if you did not murder or rape, then you are not guilty."

"But what about a child who steals a cookie?" David asked. "Is he not guilty of stealing?"

"The child was hungry and did only what he needed to do." Zay'id shrugged. "We do not use the word 'guilt' in this case."

"What do you use?" David asked.

"Nothing, the child was hungry."

"What if he does bad things?"

"Then he is acting in a shameful way. His actions will bring shame on the family. Not guilt."

David was really puzzled. "So what would I have to do to be guilty?"

Zay'id smiled. "You would have to murder me, or Mr. Li."

"What if I lied to you?" David protested. "Wouldn't I be guilty of lying?"

"We would never use guilt and lying together."

"But lying is wrong."

"That depends why you lied," Zay'id argued. "If a lie leads to a good result, then it is not wrong. If I defend the honor of my family by lying, then it is perfectly okay."

"No," David argued. "A lie is a lie. It is always wrong. You must always tell the truth."

"Even when it is harmful to you and to others?"

"Yes, I always tell the truth, even if it hurts."

"You are very strange, David."

"No, it's in the Bible. The Bible says, 'Let your yes be yes, and your no be no.'"

Zay'id turned to Mr. Li. "What is your response to this?" he asked.

"I need to think about this before I answer," Mr. Li said. "This is a very interesting topic, and it may help us understand one another better."

A few days later, the three men met in the hospital courtyard. Once again, they discussed the topic of guilt. "I've been doing some thinking and questioning on this topic," Mr. Li began. "Zay'id, if I murder someone and hide the body, and no one every finds the body, am I guilty of murder?"

"Of course not," Zay'id answered.

David's eyes got big. "But you did it."

"No one knows. No shame had been brought on my family."

"What would happen if a man kills his daughter to protect the honor of the family?" Mr. Li asked. "Is this murder?"

"Of course not," Zay'id answered again.

This was too much for David. "What do you mean?" he protested. "Killing is murder!"

Zay'id looked surprised. "No, it is not. If a man kills to protect the honor of his family, it is an honor-killing. It is perfectly acceptable."

"Murder is wrong," David protested. "It is wrong to take someone's life, anytime."

"What about war?"

"War is evil. Killing in war is a necessary evil."

"Does it make you guilty?" Zay'id asked.

"I think many soldiers feel guilty after the war is over. My grandfather struggled with guilt for the rest of his life."

"What is this feeling of guilt?" Zay'id asked. "I don't understand it."

"You know, you do something wrong, and you feel guilty."

"Ashamed?"

"No, you may also feel ashamed, especially if you are caught, but when you do something you know is wrong, then you feel guilty."

"I see," said Zay'id slowly. "To eat pork or drink wine is forbidden. But if I've never eaten pork or drank alcohol, then I will never feel guilty."

"What if you went over to that fig tree over there and stole a fig from it? Wouldn't you feel guilty?"

"Of course not."

"Why? It's not your tree. You stole!"

"God made the tree, and the fruit is for everyone."

"Isn't taking a fig from someone else's tree wrong?"

"He has lots of figs. I only want one. To be a glutton and take many would be to act shamefully."

David shook his head, bent over, and placed it in his hands. "I'm so confused. In my world, everything is either right or wrong. It's better that way. Then we know where we are."

"Who says what is right or wrong?"

"The law does. That's why we have the law."

"Who made the law?"

"I don't know. I guess the founding fathers did."

"So you live your life according to manmade laws? The whims of society? And you feel guilty when you break the laws?"

David nodded in agreement.

"I think I read somewhere that the speed limit used to be 90 km an hour across the whole of the USA."

"That's right," David answered.

"But now it is faster?" Zay'id asked.

"Yes, now we can go 120 km per hour on the main roads."

"Don't you feel guilty?" Zay'id asked with a smile.

"No, the law has changed."

Zay'id smiled larger. "Society makes laws. They change laws. You shouldn't feel guilty about breaking those laws. They are manmade."

"This is an absurd conversation," David protested. "The law is the law. I am a law-abiding citizen. That is the Christian thing to do."

Zay'id looked at Mr. Li. "I think our cultures are very different from each other."

"But mine is built on Christian principles. Yours is built on Islam. That is the difference."

Mr. Li frowned. "I think there is more here than that. My country is quite similar, and it is not Islamic. This is going to take a lot more thought. We need to pray and ask God to show us more about culture, and what his will in this matter is."

Although the three men realized that their cultures were different, they agreed to put these things aside until God showed them more about the topic.

11

David was excited when he visited Mr. Li later that week. "Guess what?" he asked excitedly. "You'll never guess what is going to happen."

"No, I have no idea." Mr. Li smiled. "What is going on?"

"Mahmoud wants to get married. He is going to ask for a girl's hand in marriage."

"That's interesting," Mr. Li commented. "I know nothing about Muslim marriages."

"Well, you had better. They have invited you to come to their house tonight."

"Really? What are they going to do?"

"I don't know, but Mahmoud's father has asked specifically for you."

"Are you also invited?"

"He didn't mention me. He just said that he wants you to come to his house tonight, right after the afternoon prayer time."

"Okay, I will arrange some time off. I am supposed to do rounds in the hospital this evening to make sure that everything is done. I will ask Ahmed. He is now taking more and more responsibility."

That evening Mr. Li dressed in his best clothes and took the bus across town to Mahmoud's house. When he arrived, a crowd of men was gathering. All of them looked very somber, and all of them were very well dressed. Mahmoud's father took Mr. Li around the circle and introduced him to some of the guests. Many of them recognized Mr. Li from the welcome back party several weeks before.

"Tonight we are going to ask for a bride for Mahmoud," someone told Mr. Li. "Most of us will just be there to represent the family. The leaders of the tribe will do all the discussing."

Mr. Li suddenly felt better. At least he would not be called upon. But he was excited to be a part of this event. There were many people there. Several Sheiks from the mosque were there, as were a couple of doctors, some lawyers, and a politician. Others were businessmen or important members of the larger family. Mr. Li was the only foreigner. David was not present.

After they had all gathered, the men got into cars. Mr. Li found himself in the back of a German Mercedes Benz. It was a very nice car, nicer than anything he had ever been in before. Every seat was packed with people, and they headed off, driving in a convoy. The drive took them about fifteen minutes. The cars pulled up before an apartment block and the men piled out. With Mahmoud's father and some of the tribal elders leading them, the men made their way into the apartment building. Mr. Li noticed people looking out of their windows to see what was happening.

The group crowded into the stairwell and the leading men knocked on an apartment door. They could hear people rushing around inside. Obviously, they had been spotted coming. The door opened, and a man inside welcomed them. They filed into the house as the family rushed to provide enough chairs. Someone dashed out to borrow some chairs from the neighbors. Soon all the men were sitting on the chairs and coffee was served. The men visited together, drank sweet tea, then more coffee. Mahmoud's father introduced everyone in the group, mentioning who they were and what their job was. Mr. Li was introduced as a friend of the family from China, working at the hospital.

After the second cup of coffee was served, the men's discussion moved to politics and world news. The evening wore on, and nothing special was happening. Finally, the third cup of coffee arrived, and the men prepared to go. They rose, said goodbye to their hosts, and started for the door. At the door, Mahmoud's father shook the hand of their host. "Thank you for your hospitality."

"You have honored us with your visit," the man replied.

"May God bless you and your house," Mahmoud's father replied.

"And your house," the man replied.

"There was one other thing," Mahmoud's father added. "We would like to ask for your daughter's hand in marriage for our son."

The man smiled. "You are honoring our family with your request. Please, let us discuss this."

All of the men returned to their seats. "Which one is Mahmoud?" the man asked. When Mahmoud was identified, he was carefully looked over.

"Have you finished school?"

"He has finished his secondary school, and one year of university," Mahmoud's father replied proudly.

"Have you prepared a house?"

"We have a wonderful apartment prepared. It has a bedroom, a sitting room, and a kitchen. Our family has furnished everything." All of the men nodded in agreement.

"What about work? Does Mahmoud have work?"

"Yes, he works with Abdullah over there. He is an engineer. Mahmoud will continue his studies next year, and his employment with Abdullah."

"I would like my daughter to decide if she will marry this man," the girl's father continued. He nodded to one of the young men standing in a doorway. A few minutes later, a very pale and nervous girl entered the room. She was strikingly beautiful, well dressed, and looked only to her father. He indicated Mahmoud. "This young man is asking for you. Are you prepared to marry?"

Her eyes dropped to the floor and then rose to look into Mahmoud's eyes. Obviously, they knew one another. She smiled shyly, then dropped her eyes and raised them only to her father. "Yes, I am ready to marry."

"And to this man?"

"As you choose, father."

"You may go" he motioned for her to leave.

"What about the dowry?" Mahmoud's father asked.

"What would you like?"

"The family is asking for four thousand dollars, plus clothing and gold for the bride."

At this, the men turned to each other in amazement. "Four thousand?" they whispered. This was apparently a lot of money.

"You are an honorable family," the man continued. "You have many well-placed men, I'm sure four thousand is nothing to a family such as yourself."

Several of the men muttered under their breaths; if every bride cost four thousand, then the family would soon be broke.

After some negotiations, the tribal leaders settled on a two-thousand-dollar dowry, a new wardrobe for the girl, and a half kilogram of gold. The latter surprised Mr. Li, for it the gold would be quite expensive. Eventually, everyone shook hands with everyone, and they prepared to go.

"Before you leave, we must drink coffee to seal the agreement," the girl's father insisted.

Small coffee cups were circulated and the men each downed the 1/3 cup before passing the cups back to their host, who refilled them and passed them on to others.

It was several months before the wedding took place. Mr. Li visited Mahmoud's family several times and was present when the engagement party took place. It was a great celebration, as the girl was not from the immediate tribe, but one more distantly related to Mahmoud's family. The event signaled stronger relations between the two tribes.

On the day of the wedding, Mahmoud's father invited Mr. Li to be present during the preparations. He arrived early in the morning as the men were preparing to slaughter several sheep. The sheep arrived in the back seat of someone's car and were taken up onto the flat roof of the apartment building. The four men ate a little bread and drank tea while they decided what they should do. Then Mr. Li accompanied the men upstairs to where the sheep were kept and together they brought them down to the side of the street to be killed. One man produced a knife and looked around to see which way he should face. Once they had determined which direction Mecca was, the sheep were faced in that direction, and one by one their throats were slit, while the man said, "in the name of Allah, the compassionate and merciful."

The second man took the dead sheep and made a small hole in the skin. Then he started blowing air into the hole. Slowly, the sheep started to expand. Mr. Li watched in amazement as the sheep grew larger and large. Eventually, the man stopped and went to the next sheep and started doing the same. Suddenly Mr. Li understood. The air had forced the sheep's skin to separate from the body. The men now skinned the sheep and hung them up to drain. Then they opened the body cavity and took out the innards. They looked around with worried looks and hurriedly placed them in a plastic bag. Once all of the guts were in the bag, they rushed to one of the cars. Mr. Li jumped in with two of the men and they sped off. One man remained to continue working with the sheep.

Mr. Li wondered where they were going. They drove out of the city and along a narrow road into the desert. Finally, they turned off the road onto a dirt track. "There's a good place," one of them suggested. "Too close to the road," the other one answered. They continued driving another ten minutes. "How about over that small embankment?" one of them asked. They stopped the car and removed a shovel from the trunk. After a shallow hole had been dug, they dropped the large plastic bag into it and covered it with dirt.

"Why didn't we just throw the bag into the big garbage dumpster in town?" Mr. Li asked. "Why did you bring it all the way out here?"

The men exchanged glances. "Well, it's because of the women," one answered.

Mr. Li waited for an explanation. He looked from one to the other. "The women do stuff," the other man explained. "They take the insides of the sheep and make spells, or medicine, to affect people."

Mr. Li looked puzzled. "Isn't medicine good?"

"Not in this case. They can put a spell on you or make you sick. There are many things they can do if they have animal parts. So we get rid of the parts as fast as possible, where no women will find them."

As they drove back to the house, Mr. Li sat in the back seat. He wondered about what had taken place. "If a woman makes a spell, is there anything that will protect you?"

"This," one of the men said, picking up a small Qur'an from off of the car dashboard. "This will protect you. You carry it in your pocket."

"Or," the other man added, "on the dash of your car. It protects us from accidents."

Mr. Li was surprised. He had seen many Qur'ans in vehicles, but he had never realized that people thought of them as protection.

"Is there anything else?" He asked.

"There are lots of things that can protect you. But you have to go to someone who has the power. See that car over there?" Mr. Li nodded. "See underneath the car? There is a small child's shoe hanging down?" Mr. Li had seen this several times but wasn't sure what it meant. "The person with power had made the shoe powerful, so it will protect the driver from hitting a small child."

"Really?"

"Yes, that is why the sign of a hand is used. The hand of Fatima, it is the sign of a hand with the image of an eye drawn in the middle."

"I've seen that. What does that mean?"

"It protects you from the evil eye."

"The evil eye! What is that?"

"If someone looks at you with jealousy in their eye, a curse can be put upon you. Or perhaps the spirits become jealous of you if you have something nice."

"That's why we like the color green," the other man explained. "It helps keep the evil eye away."

Mr. Li was surprised at how superstitious these men were. He hadn't realized it until this day. "You mentioned spirits. Do spirits harm you?"

"Yes, spirits can do many things to you. They can trip you and throw you to the ground while you are walking."

"Or," the other man added, "they can sit on you at night and choke you."

"Sometimes," the first man added, "they make you very nervous."

"Have you seen this?"

"Yes, my sister was attacked last year!"

"Really!?" Mr. Li asked. "What happened?"

"She threw out water."

Mr. Li was very puzzled. "What does that mean?"

"You know, she threw out water."

"So? I don't understand."

The first man looked exasperated. "Before water hits the ground, you must say 'In the name of Allah' or the demons will jump up from the ground and attack you. Everyone knows this."

"I've never heard of this," Mr. Li responded.

"Don't the demons attack you in China?" the man asked. "What do you say when you urinate? How do you keep from being attacked?"

"We don't have this problem."

The two men exchanged puzzled glances. "Perhaps it is because your country is not a desert country. Perhaps it is only desert spirits who do this."

By this time, they had arrived back at the house, and preparations were being made for the wedding. A large tent was erected, and a truckload of plastic chairs were unloaded and arranged around the tent. The men then went to change into their best clothing. Soon, a large group of men from the groom's tribe gathered. With Mahmoud and his closest cousins leading the way, the men got into cars and the back of pickup trucks. They drove to near the girl's house. Once they had assembled on the street, they began to walk together towards the house. The men broke out into singing. It was a happy occasion. They were coming to get the bride and take her back to their home. She would become part of their tribe now, and her children would be the children of their tribe.

12

David's taxi screeched to a halt. Lying in the middle of the street was a teen-age girl, dying. She had been shot in the head four times. Just then her brother walked across the street with two policemen and stated, "there she is. I killed her because she was in an immoral situation with a man."

David was shocked. His face was pale and his hands shook until his taxi dropped him at the hospital. A few minutes later, he was in Mr. Li's room together with Zay'id. "I cannot go on living here in this country," he complained. "These people are barbarians. How can a young man kill his sister? These people are murderers!"

Zay'id smiled. "Are you calling me a barbarian?"

"How can a boy kill his sister?"

"It was an honor killing. She had dishonored the entire family. His family asked him to do it."

David looked at him with uncomprehending eyes. "His family?" he asked. "His entire family was behind it?"

"Yes, it is the law in our country. The young man is innocent. He did not commit murder; he only preserved the honor of his family."

"This is absurd," David protested.

"Let me tell you a story from my tribe," Zay'id said gently, sitting down on the bed. "Some years ago, a cousin of mine, a beautiful young girl, ran away from home. We didn't know where she was. Some weeks later, our family learned she had married someone from another religion. Everyone in our family was furious. The police imprisoned the girl so that she would be protected from us. Our family met, and our grandmothers taunted her brothers and father. 'How long do we need to keep our heads to the ground in shame? Won't you do something to cleanse the shame from our tribe so we can raise our heads and live in honor once again?' Then our family agreed to pay the police a $50,000.00 guarantee that we would not hurt her, and she was released into our custody. Within hours, her father and brothers shot her thirteen times. The entire family was pleased that honor had been restored.

"No," David groaned, covering his ears. "I thought you people were all nice people. I thought I liked it here."

"What has changed?" Mr. Li asked gently.

"Everything!" David protested. "This is all wrong. It's wrong and evil."

"I think it has to do with culture," Mr. Li said. "Some cultures are more sensitive to shame than other cultures."

"Shame? What is this about shame?" David asked. "It was wrong."

"That's exactly what I mean. The Muslims see it as shame, you see it as wrong. But both are looking at the same thing. I believe that we are going to have to learn a lot more about shame and guilt, as we seem to be disagreeing on this subject quite often."

"Is this really an important topic?" David asked.

"Yes, you explain the gospel as God dealing with their guilt. Zay'id sees it as God dealing with his shame."

"Why would God deal with his shame? Guilt is all that matters. Shame is what others think of you."

"I believe it is more than that. Let's ask God to show us more about this topic this week."

Every night, David would drop by the post-office to collect mail for himself and other members of his missions team. They all shared the same postbox, and it was David's job to get the mail, since he lived closest to the post office. Every night he would descend the stairs from the hillside where he lived, make his way through the market, and then go into the post office. Every night, he would greet the soldier who was there to guard the post office and make sure that it was kept clean.

That week, however, David noticed that there was no guard. Instead, a middle-aged man in a business suit sat in the soldier's chair. David greeted him and went to his post-box. The businessman watched him closely, leaning far back in his chair to watch him take out his mail. As he was leaving, it seemed to David that the businessman wanted to say something, but nothing was said as they passed each other. David thought nothing about this until the following evening when the businessman was back, sitting in the soldier's chair.

As David entered, the businessman rose, greeted David, and shook his hand. David greeted him back and then proceeded to his mailbox. The businessman followed.

"Excuse me," the man said, "but do you get your mail from box 1936?"

"Yes," David answered. He was puzzled about what might be wrong. The door of the post box looked strong and okay. Nothing seemed to be wrong.

"Could I talk with you a few moments?" the man asked. He motioned towards the two plastic chairs by the doorway. "I'm sorry to trouble you," the man began. "I am not a soldier. I don't work here. I asked the soldier if I could be here because I wanted to see who gets mail from that postbox."

David looked confused, so the man continued. "I work inside the post office. My job is to open mail and read it, to check what is going in and out of the country. I've been reading the mail that people get in that postbox and I have some questions."

David tried not to look alarmed. This man obviously worked for the secret police, or some government intelligence agency. "I will try and answer your questions," he said meekly.

"Who is Isaiah?"

"What?"

"Who is Isaiah? I've seen people quote him in letters, and I wondered who he was."

"Oh!" David was surprised. "He is one of the prophets."

"The prophets? I thought all the writings of the prophets were lost."

"No, the writings of the prophets have been preserved. We have all the writings of the prophets from Moses to Jesus."

The policeman looked puzzled. "All of the letters to this postbox are in English. Do these writings exist in my language as well?"

"Yes," David brightened. "I can get you a book with the writings of the prophets, plus the Injil. Would you like a copy?" David knew that Injil is the word for the Gospels, as understood in Islam.

David arranged to meet the policeman, who introduced himself as Mohammad, the next evening. He rushed home and prepared his present and the next day delivered it to him.

Several days later, the policeman was back at the post office waiting for David. He explained that he was having trouble understanding what he was reading, so he and David arranged to meet several times a week to discuss the Bible.

One night, several weeks later, Mohammed arrived at David's house, obviously agitated. After the traditional cup of tea, Mohammed closed the windows to David's living room, and sat close beside him, speaking almost in a whisper. Mohammed seemed afraid and said, "The walls may have ears."

As they huddled together, he quietly explained he had a problem with a Bible passage. His reading of the Bible had progressed smoothly until he had arrived at I Samuel 2:8. It was Hannah's song of praise to God for giving her her son Samuel. When Mohammed arrived at verse 8, he found something that he couldn't cope with. Hannah said, "He raises the poor from the dust and lifts up the beggars from the dunghill; He seats them with princes and has them inherit a throne of honor," as it was rendered in the Arabic Bible.

Mohammed threw the Bible down on the coffee table. "No," he said emphatically. "This cannot be true. A beggar is a beggar; a prince is a prince. This is garbage."

As David stared at Mohammed's face, he suddenly saw a truth he had never seen before. This wasn't garbage; this was the Gospel. I Samuel 2:8 described the Gospel in the terms of God taking us from the shame of sin and raising us to being joint heirs with Christ.

He tried explaining it to Mohammed. "No," Muhammad protested. "You cannot move from shame to honor. If you are born the son of a thief, then you will be a thief. The daughter of a prostitute will be a prostitute. They do not become kings and queens."

Silently, David was praying hard, asking God to provide him with an answer for Mohammad's questions.

"Do you like Australians?" David asked, startled that the words came out of his mouth.

"Yes, Australians are fine people." Mohammad answered.

"Are they really?" David asked.

"Yes, I have an uncle who emigrated to Australia. He said that Australians are very good people."

"What do you know about Australians?" David now knew why the Lord had put the question in his mouth.

"I don't know much about them. Why?"

"You should learn about the history of Australia. At one time, it was a giant prison for England. That was where they sent all the thieves and prostitutes."

"It cannot be," Mohammad gasped.

"But people change. Christians went there to reach the people, and today Australians are nice people. I agree. But long ago many were changed by the gospel."

This was too much for Mohammad. "I cannot believe this," he said, rising to leave. "Thank you for the tea."

Several nights later, Mohammad was back. "You were right," he said after they had sat down for another study. "I checked about the history of Australia, and you are right." He looked amazed. "It really is possible for people to change. We Muslims always say that people cannot change."

"Without God's help, it really is very hard to change." David smiled. "But with God, all things are possible. Do you want to see where it tells us this in the Bible?"

13

David held a letter in his lands. Mr. Li and Zay'id sat across from him, listening. "My parents are really worried about me. They have always been concerned about the Muslim country I live in."

"What is it that they are concerned about?" Mr. Li asked.

"Terrorists," David replied. "They are afraid of Muslim terrorists. They think that every Muslim is a terrorist."

"Can you not tell them that people here are like people everywhere in the world?" Zay'id asked.

"I've tried, but they are convinced that Muslims are basically bad people. I've even tried inviting them to visit me, but they are too afraid."

Zay'id looked puzzled. "That is very interesting. My parents also think that Christian's are bad people."

"Really?" David looked surprised. "Why would they think that? Christians are almost all good people. There might be a few bad ones once in a while, but generally we are all pretty good people."

"That is not what Muslims believe."

"How can that be?"

"Muslims believe that America, Britain, Canada, and other countries are Christian countries."

"I can see where they got that from. Our countries were founded on Christian principles, often by Christians, or at least nominal Christians who held good Christian principles."

"Therefore," Zay'id continued, the problems you have in America are Christian problems."

"Like what?"

"Alcoholism. Muslims do not drink alcohol."

David looked puzzled.

"Pornography. This is a western problem. We don't allow it in our countries." Zay'id paused. "We don't have homeless people. We don't have prostitutes on the street. We don't have drug addicts on our street. These are all Christian problems."

"It's not true," David protested.

"My people are not terrorists either."

"You are right. But my parents think that everyone here is bad because they are Muslims."

"And my parents think that the system in America is bad, because of the bad results it produces in society."

David shook his head. "What a crazy world we live in!"

Zay'id was now getting excited. "When I was growing up, we heard that churches were bad places."

"Really?" David was puzzled again. "How could that be?"

"We heard all sorts of stories about churches. We heard that Christians drowned babies in churches."

"I can understand that. There are some churches that baptize babies. Maybe it came from that."

Zay'id eyes got big. "We heard that Christians ate human flesh and drank blood."

"This I can understand," Mr. Li added. "They just didn't understand the Lord's Supper."

"When I was a boy," Zay'id continued, "my friends and I heard about all kinds of sexual things that happened in churches. One night, the Christians were having a party. I think it was called a New Year's party. We sat outside the church, across the street, and watched and listened. They were playing music, eating, and drinking and having a party inside. Men and women were freely mixing together and laughing and joking. Then, around midnight, they turned out the lights. We could see only a couple of candles glowing. The men and women were all together in a dark room. There were strange noises, like whisperings and groaning. It went on for twenty or thirty minutes. Later, they turned the lights back on. There was no more laughter, and everyone went home without talking to their neighbors." There was a long pause as David and Mr. Li imagined what Zay'id had seen. "Tell me that this wasn't an orgy. I saw it with my own eyes."

David shook his head sadly. "Zay'id, you saw a typical Christian New Year's party. Christian men and women mix more freely than Muslims do. Then, at midnight, the pastor would have called them together to pray. They must have had a candle-lit service. What you heard were men and women praying to God for the New Year. It wouldn't have been anything sexual."

Zay'id looked from one to the other. "But what we saw..." he began. "To us, it looked like bad things were happening. We told it all over the town. Everyone learned about it."

"No wonder people throw stones at the church," David commented.

"Christians are also plotting to take over the world," Zay'id continued. "This is why America is invading countries. This is why they support the country of Israel. The Jews and the Christians are plotting to rule the world." He looked triumphant. "We've heard that they have guns buried under churches, and that their young people go to special military training camps in the summer."

David shook his head in disbelief.

"We've heard that Christians are training thousands of special missionaries to invade our countries and force Muslims to convert to Christianity. We've heard that they will first entice us with money, gifts, university scholarships, even women, if we will convert. But no true Muslim has ever left the faith. And if some weak person does, there are followers of Islam that will protect the honor of Islam and remove them."

David held his head in his hands. "God, please help us. How can we ever share the good news with these people?"

14

The hospital was strangely empty and quiet one evening as Mr. Li did his rounds. No one moved in the hallways, and even the nurses were not at their desks. A few patients were in their beds, but many of the beds were empty.

"*Where is everyone?*" Mr. Li wondered as he walked down the halls. The place was almost deserted. Had something happened? And then he heard a noise. It sounded like a crowd of people talking. Suddenly, they were quiet again. Rounding a corner, Mr. Li came to the television room. A large group of people were crowded into the room, listening to the television. Doctors, nurses, and patients crowded around the TV. The program was in the local language, so it was hard for Mr. Li to understand. He was standing at the back of the crowd, trying to listen to what was going on. It appeared to be a normal TV story.

A young man was talking on a cell phone. "Hello," he said in a gruff voice. "This is Mr. Tarik. I'm Muhammad's uncle on his father's side." People in the room started laughing and chuckling. "I'm calling about his application for work. You did receive it, didn't you? ... Yes... I want to encourage you to hire him. He is an excellent worker, and our whole family stands behind him." There was more laughter. "Yes, our whole family stands in support of him. He is an exceptional worker. You will be most pleased with him... yes... okay, here is my phone number." The young man gave a phone number and then hung up. He walked nervously around the room. He jumped when his phone suddenly rang. "Hello," he shouted. "Yes, you want Mr. Tarik. Just a moment." He looked wildly around. "Dad, it's for you," he shouted. Everyone in the room laughed. The young man stomped his feet on the ground and then raised the phone to his ear and gruffly said, "hello this is Mr. Tarik." People in the crowded room chuckled and giggled.

"Yes, thank you for calling back. I understand. Thank you. I'm sure he will do just fine. If there are any issues, please call me and I will do whatever I can to help you. Thank you. Bye."

The young man on the television hung up the phone and started dancing and jumping around. Music started playing, and it was obvious the TV show was over. Everyone started getting up and going back to work. Mr. Li spotted Ahmed, one of his workers, in the crowd.

"What is going on?" he asked. "Why was everyone watching that TV show?"

"Haven't you heard?" Ahmed smiled. "It's the new TV drama about Muhammad, a man without a family."

"Yes," Mr. Li said. "Why is everyone so excited?"

"Because he has no family," Ahmed said emphatically. "He has no one to help him get a job, rent an apartment, buy a car, get a wife."

"Yes," Mr. Li continued. "What else?"

"What else?" Ahmed looked incredulous. "That's it. It's a great story. He has to do everything himself. His family has either died or emigrated and he is all alone. He has to do everything himself. It's a great story. Everyone is watching it."

By now, the hospital had returned to its normal state, and people were working and talking. Everywhere Mr. Li went, as he inspected the work his cleaning crew had done, he heard people talking about the television show. It had apparently made a great impact on everyone. The following evening, Mr. Li was out buying groceries when the streets suddenly went quiet. He waited for a long time for a taxi to come by. It seemed that there were very few cars on the road.

"Where is everyone tonight?" he asked the taxi driver. "I had to wait a long time for a taxi to come by."

"It's that new TV program," the taxi driver said. "Everyone is watching it."

"Yes, it seems like the whole country shuts down for it."

"Things will be back to normal when it is over." The driver commented. And indeed, it was true. No sooner had Mr. Li made it back to the workers' compound at the hospital, when people started moving around again, and things seemed normal. Everyone, however, was talking about the TV show. It seemed that in tonight's program, young Muhammad was having difficulties remembering who he was supposed to be on the telephone. And now he needed to pretend he was one of his aunts. Everyone was laughing about how well he could mimic a woman's voice.

The following evening, after the TV show was over, Mr. Li met with David and Ahmed in his room for tea. "This really is a popular program," Mr. Li started.

"Yes," Ahmed answered. "This is one of the best TV programs that's been on in a long time. Everyone will be sad when it is over tomorrow evening. I wonder how it will end."

"It is really very strange," David commented. "I don't really understand what the appeal is. It seems like a rather foolish program to me."

"That is because you are not one of us," Ahmed commented. "You live alone. Your family is far away, and you have to do everything yourself. That would be very difficult for us. Students do it, but we rely on our families to help us."

"This I have seen," Mr. Li commented. "The family members all support one another. It is very admirable."

"It is our way," Ahmed said proudly. "Don't you also have tribes?"

David shook his head. "I know who some of my cousins are, but I don't know my other relatives. Most of my relatives I've never met or I've only seen at a family reunion or wedding. My family isn't very close. We live all over the USA."

"This is very strange," Ahmed commented.

"No, I don't think so," David countered. "In America, most of our family roots go back to someone who immigrated to America long ago. They usually left the old world, and we don't have any contact with the old families across the ocean. So most of us don't really think in terms of family, except our immediate family."

"And if you need your family for something..?"

"We do it ourselves. Americans are individuals. We like to be independent," David said proudly.

It was Ahmed's time to shake his head. "Americans and Muslims are exact opposites. No wonder there is so much trouble between us."

The following week, Mr. Li and David resumed their quest to discover more about the Muslim opinion of honor and shame. They asked Zay'id to help them. Zay'id was at first reluctant to talk about his culture, but in the end, he agreed.

"Can you tell us about shameful acts?" David asked. "What sort of things could you do that would put you in a position of shame before your family?"

"Anything that embarrasses my family would be shameful," he responded. "But most families are lenient with young men. After all, we are just young guys messing around. They figure once we get a good Muslim wife, we will settle down. Then, once we have children and play a responsible role in the tribe, we will be much better behaved. So, boys will be boys."

"So, is there anything you could do that would cause your family to react with anger and perhaps kill you?"

"Well, they might throw me out of the tribe if I did something really terrible that embarrassed them all. But the only reason they might kill me is if I publicly renounced Islam. If that happened, then everyone would put pressure on them and they would take my life."

"Wow," David responded. "You must be afraid that anything you might do would bring dishonor on your tribe."

"No, most men are safe," Zay'id responded. "It is the women who must be careful. A woman can easily bring shame on her family. She must always be careful never to put herself into a position that could be interpreted negatively."

"Like what?"

"Like being alone with a man she is not married to. People would talk. And talk would lead to shame."

"You mean she doesn't have to commit a bad act?"

"No, she simply has to be suspected of the act."

"That is amazing," David responded. "If a woman came over to my house and I invited her in, she would be bringing shame on her family?"

"She wouldn't even have to come into your house," Zay'id responded.

"I don't understand."

"It is enough to walk alone on the street with no family members with her. That alone would put her into a position of shame."

"But I've seen women alone on the street."

"Did they have someone with them, even a child?"

"You are right. Women always have someone with them," David responded. "But this once I remember seeing a woman on the street. She looked right into my eyes as well."

"That," Zay'id smiled, "is the sign of a prostitute. She walks alone and is bold enough to look you in the eyes."

"Wait," Mr. Li said. "Now I understand why women never talk to me and never look at me. They always look away when they talk to me."

"They are being proper women," Zay'id responded. "Many women are even afraid to take a job at the hospital, because it puts them in situations where there is no family member around to witness their behavior. People might talk."

"Okay," David responded. "Tell me this. I've always heard about Muslim men keeping women in a harem. How does this fit?"

"Most westerners have the wrong view of the harem," Zay'id replied. "The harem is part of the house where the women are. The word Harem comes from 'harram' meaning forbidden. This is especially true in large houses. Their side of the house is forbidden to men. They live there in complete protection with the children."

"What happens when a boy grows up?" Mr. Li asked.

"When a boy starts to notice girls," Zay'id smiled, "then we have a special ceremony, and he joins the men's side of the house."

"So men never go into the harem?" David asked.

"Never. A woman is always totally safe in the harem."

"So how does a married man... you know..." David said, obviously embarrassed to continue.

"What?" Zay'id teased.

"How does he have relations with his wife?"

"He may have more than one wife in the harem. All the women of the house live together. Mothers, grandmothers, wives, and so on. When he wants to spend time with one of his wives, he requests to see her in one of the rooms that separate the men's side of the house from the women's."

"This is amazing. Are all homes like this?"

"No, only the traditional ones. Now in the city, everything is different."

"So men don't have harems in the city?"

"No, if a man wants more than one wife, he usually rents an apartment for each wife and her children and moves around between them," Zay'id explained. "It is a great honor for a man to have more than one wife. Four is even better. Islam allows us to have four wives."

Just then Ahmed came to the door. "Does anyone want to go to the coffeehouse with me?" he asked. "Kaldun, the famous storyteller, will be there tonight."

"What is a storyteller?" David asked.

"Storytellers go from place to place telling the famous old stories. They really are very good," Zay'id answered. "If you want to learn about our country, you should go."

"Okay," David shrugged. "Are you going to come too?"

"Sure," Mr. Li responded. "I've never heard a storyteller."

When they arrived at the coffee-house, a crowd had gathered. They eventually found places at a low table and paid for their coffees. The place was noisy and smoky. Men crowded around small tables, sitting on chairs and boxes. The man behind the counter poured thick boiling sweet coffee into small cups which were set before the men. After some time, it was announced that Kaldun had arrived. He was an older man, with small glasses and a loud voice. He greeted everyone with a wave of his hand: "peace be unto you," and all the men responded, "and peace be unto you."

Kaldun seated himself on a high stool and accepted a cup of hot, sticky coffee. He waited for a few minutes, speaking to a few individuals he knew, and then he began his story. He accompanied the story with hand gestures, wide eyes, and emotion. David listened closely:

"a Sheik, an honorable man of his tribe, was traveling across the desert. The Sheik became very tired at noon day and so when he came to some trees, he sought out the cool shade of a palm tree and lay down. He carefully took off his outer robe, a special robe that denoted his importance in the tribe, with embroidery and gold trim, folded it, and lay it carefully beside him. Then he fell asleep.

"While he was sleeping, a poor man happened to come by. He saw the Sheik asleep under the tree and the gold embroidered robe laying beside him. Very carefully, walking as gently as a cat, he came up to the Sheik and picked up the robe. Then, walking backwards, he quietly withdrew and went on his way.

"After some time, as the sun continued its way across the sky, the shadow moved, and the Sheik became uncomfortably warm. He woke up and wanted to continue his journey." The storyteller stopped to sip his coffee. The men all leaned forward to hear what would happen next. Some were smiling. They had probably heard the story before.

"'Eyyyii!' the Sheik cried when he realized that his robe had been stolen. His honorable robe, that demonstrated to everyone his place in the tribe, had been robbed from him. Hurriedly he made his way home, afraid that people would see him in his position of disgrace. At home, he sulked and complained about what had happened.

"The young men of his family decided that the tribal honor must be maintained. From their home, they moved out across the desert, visiting village after village to see if they could find the missing robe. And sure enough, in one town they found the thief in the market, trying to sell the robe. They grabbed the man and were going to kill him when soldiers arrived and demanded that they all appear before the magistrate.

"Someone was sent back for the old Sheik. When he arrived, everyone was gathered before the magistrate. The judge turned to the Sheik and asked him to tell his part of the story.

"'I was traveling across the desert,' the Sheik said, 'and when I was tired I went to sleep under a tree. Before I slept, I folded my robe and placed it beside me. When I awoke, my robe had been stolen.'

"'And is this your robe?' the magistrate asked.

"'Yes, this is my robe.'

"'Well,' the magistrate said, turning to the thief, 'what do you have to say for yourself?'

"'The Sheik speaks the truth,' the thief said. 'I was traveling across the desert, and came to the grove of trees. There I saw a man asleep under a tree. So I went over and had sex with him while he slept. I then took his robe and left.'

"'Wait!' the Sheik cried, 'let me see that robe again. No, it is not my robe. I was mistaken.' The thief went free."

The men in the restaurant howled with laughter and applauded. More coffee was served, and everyone was talking at once.

David simply shook his head in disbelief. He looked at Mr. Li, who spread his hands. He didn't know what to make of it, either.

15

The crowd at the coffeehouse enjoyed the stories that Kaldun told. Business was good for the owner of the coffee shop, as people ordered tea and coffee, nuts and seeds, and cigarettes.

After a short break, the storyteller began again:

"there once was a very poor man. When the noon meal came, he had only a few small coins to buy something with. He was very hungry, but could only afford a piece of bread. Approaching a street café, he asked if he could buy one piece of bread. The owner of the store was not very happy with such a poorly dressed man standing in front of his restaurant. 'Here,' he said, 'take this piece of bread and go away.'

"The man paid his last coins for the bread, and moved away from the front of the restaurant, where one of the workers was cooking meat over hot coals. It smelled very good. The poor man desperately wanted to buy some meat, but he had no money, so he stood downwind from the cooking meat, and every time he took a bite of his bread, he breathed deeply, so he could smell the meat.

"The owner called for him to move, but the poor man stood his ground and ate his bread. He was out of the way, and he was enjoying the smell of the meat. This outraged the owner, and so he called for the police to come and arrest the man. The police told the owner that he should come with them as well, so he could state his case against the poor man.

"A few moments later, the men were ushered before the magistrate, who asked the owner to state his case. At the end, the magistrate was amazed. 'You brought this man here for smelling your meat cooking?' he asked.

"'Yes,' the owner said. 'I asked him to move, and he did not.'

"'And what is your story?' the magistrate asked the poor man.

"'The owner is correct,' the poor man answered. 'I had only enough money to buy bread. After I bought the bread, the owner asked me to leave. So I went and stood in front of the neighboring store and ate my bread.'

"'Did you smell the meat while you were eating?' the magistrate asked.

"'Yes, your honor.'

"'Then I fine you the price of a dish of meat,' the magistrate replied. "Can you pay?'

"'No,' replied the poor man. 'I have no money.'

"'Bring me two dinars in change,' the judge called out. 'Make sure they are small coins.'

"A few minutes later, a court worker came with a bag of coins. 'Stand beside the café owner,' the magistrate commanded. 'Shake the bag so he can hear the coins rattle.' Turning to the café owner, the magistrate explained, "the sound of these coins is your payment for the smell of the meat cooking."'

The men in the coffee-house laughed and applauded. The storyteller turned to his own coffee and everyone began to talk. A few minutes later, someone called out for another story:

"there once was a great sultan who ruled over a great kingdom. He had a beautiful wife whom he loved dearly. As the sultan, he could have any woman in the kingdom he desired, but his wife was the love of his heart. Everything was fine, except for one thing: no children were coming from their marriage. It was a thing that saddened the royal couple, and indeed the entire nation.

"One day, as the Sultan's wife was making her way through the market, she spotted a young girl with a newborn baby beside her. The sultan's wife looked closer at the baby. It was a beautiful child.

"The young girl looked up and saw the richly dressed woman looking at her. 'Do you want this baby?' she asked. 'I have no money. I cannot take care of him.'

"The sultan's wife was filled with compassion, and she nodded. Within a few minutes, she was whisking the child away to the palace.

"At first the Sultan was very concerned, but later he realized that his wife was completely taken up with the baby. The baby was everything that she ever wanted, except it was not her own. After a while, the Sultan grew used to the idea of the child, and eventually he took a liking to the young lad. Over the years, the baby grew up in the palace. He had the best of everything. The finest clothing, the best education, and the loving care of his adopted parent. All this time, the sultan and his wife never inquired about who the young girl was, or the origin of the baby. If they had, they would have learned that the girl had been raped by her father, who was a notorious thief and criminal.

"Eventually, the child grew into a strong young man. He moved around the palace freely, and everyone enjoyed him. However, when he turned 18, his mother decided to tell him his true identity. After a special meal in his honor, the Sultan and his wife revealed to him that they were not his true parents. He had been obtained from a young girl in the market who gave him away. They assured him that they loved him and that he would have whatever he needed. He could pursue any career he chose.

"That night, the young man crept through the palace, stealing gold and silver. He raped a girl, a palace attendant, and then ran off into the night with his loot."

The story-teller looked at the crowd. "Who can tell me the proverb that illustrates the truth behind this story?"

"I know," one man shouted out. "The son of a thief is always a thief, and the daughter of a prostitute will be a prostitute." The men clapped their hands and turned again to their coffee. After a long break, they called for another story:

"a father went to work in the field one day, and he took his two sons along with him. They sat under a large tree to play while their father worked. During the day, the sun became very hot, and the father asked the older of the two boys to get him some water. 'No, I will not,' the elder son replied. The father returned to his work, but a few minutes later asked his younger son. 'Yes, certainly father,' the younger replied, but he continued playing and did not get the water."

At this point, the storyteller turned to his audience, "which is the better son?" To give the wrong answer would be shameful for the one who answered, but the storyteller knew that his listeners would give the correct answer.

"The younger son is the better of the two because he had saved his father's face by not defying him," someone in the crowd shouted out.

"Correct," the storyteller cried out, "give that man a free coffee."

After a few minutes, Mr. Li, Ahmed, and David left the coffee shop and began walking home.

"What did you think of Kaldun, the story-teller?" Ahmed asked.

"He was good," David replied, "but I cannot figure out the last story. In my opinion both boys were equally wrong."

"That wasn't the question," Mr. Li said quietly. "The story-teller asked which son was better."

"Neither was better."

"If you are only thinking of right and wrong, then you are right. To say no to your father's face would be to dishonor him. To agree with him while in front of him is to honor him. The son who honored his father was better. It wasn't a question about right and wrong."

"Isn't there a similar story in the Bible?" David asked.

"Yes," Mr. Li replied. "It is the gospel of Matthew, but I think it is a bit different. I have my New Testament here. Let's read it."

They stopped for a moment and opened the Bible to Matthew 21:28-31:

"what do you think? There was a man who had two sons. He went to the first and said, 'Son, go and work today in the vineyard.' 'I will not,' he answered, but later he changed his mind and went. Then the father went to the other son and said the same thing. He answered, 'I will, sir,' but he did not go. 'Which of the two did what his father wanted?' 'The first,' they answered. Jesus said to them "I tell you the truth, the tax collectors and the prostitutes are entering the kingdom of God ahead of you."

"What was the point of Jesus' story?" Mr. Li asked.

"I think the story is about obedience, not honor," David replied.

"Yes, and the first son, even though he dishonored his father initially, eventually obeyed him. What is Jesus teaching here?"

"Obedience is an answer to shame."

"Yes, I think it might be saying that. God desires obedience, even if we initially shame him. That is why the thieving tax collectors and prostitutes enter the kingdom of God. They received the good news of salvation and their lives changed."

Ahmed listened carefully to what they were saying about thieves and prostitutes. He didn't comment, but he was thoughtful as they walked home.

16

Night had fallen when Mr. Li's taxi made its way through the rain. Neon signs flashed in the night as they drove down the deserted main streets of the city. "There," he said to the taxi driver, pointing to a large building on the right. The sign above it said 'Housing Bank.' He paid the driver and got out into the rain. Looking both ways up the street he stepped into the doorway where there was some shelter from the rain. The bank was locked and few people were venturing out into the night.

A few minutes later another taxi pulled up, and David soon emerged. He was carrying an umbrella. Together they crowded under the umbrella and began walking up the street. "The Smiths live just around the corner," David said as they walked carefully between the streams of water that ran from downspouts onto the sidewalk. After a few minutes, they entered an apartment block and made their way up to the fourth floor and into the Smith's apartment.

Mr. and Mrs. Smith were a nice Canadian couple. They were pleased to see David, and were particularly interested in Mr. Li. "We've heard so much about you," Mrs. Smith gushed as soon as they were seated on a beautiful sofa. "David thinks very highly of you."

"I'm sure he has been very generous with his comments," Mr. Li smiled. "I hope I don't disappoint you."

"We're very glad you could come," said Mr. Smith somberly. "We are at a loss with what to do with Mona. Her case is quite complicated."

Mr. Li nodded, remembering the young woman who had approached him outside the hospital months before. "How is she? And Anna?"

"Anna has been meeting with Mona and sharing the gospel with her. Mona is very close to accepting Christ. But her situation is very difficult. She told us that we could tell you her story. She is coming here in a few moments," Mr. Smith said. He looked over at his wife. "Why don't you tell him?"

She nodded solemnly. "Mona's case is very complicated," Mrs. Smith continued. "She doesn't want people to know her story. However, she is asking for help. She has said that you two can know her case as long as you don't tell others." Mr. Li and David exchanged glances and nodded. "She is so afraid that you will be disgusted with her and throw her out. We have assured her that Christians will love her and care for her."

"You had better get started dear," her husband urged. "She is going to be here any minute."

"Okay, here is the short version of her story. A year ago, Mona became pregnant. She was not married. The father of the child was her older brother." Mrs. Smith paused and dabbed her eyes with a tissue. "When the family discovered it, they were very angry with her, and took her to a doctor in another city. He performed an abortion. After she had recovered, they took her to another doctor who did an operation and restored her virginity. Then the family wanted to quickly marry her off. There was a young man who was interested, but he soon suspected something was wrong because they were pushing so strong and rushing things. He backed down, and since then no one has come forward to ask for her. Since it is known that one man backed down, others may be afraid to ask for her. Now she is afraid that her chances of marriage are spoiled. Her family is very angry with her and she is upset with herself. She desperately wants help." Mrs. Smith paused. "She heard you tell the story of the prodigal son once and she was deeply moved. So we thought you might be the person to help her, and also give us some ideas—"

Before she could finish, the doorbell rang. Mrs. Smith rose and stepped to the door, looking out the small peep hole. "They are here," she said softly and opened the door. Anna entered first, followed by Mona. Mr. Li barely recognized her. She was much thinner, and her face drawn and taught. She had a nervous look about her. When her eyes met Mr. Li's she blushed and looked down, but not before Mr. Li had seen a silent cry for help in them.

After they were seated, Mrs. Smith served cups of hot tea to everyone and then sat down herself. "I've just explained your situation to Mr. Li and David," she began. Mona nodded and looked down. There were tears in her eyes. "I've asked Mr. Li for his advice."

Mr. Li looked calm, but on the inside, his mind was in a panic. What could he do? What should he say? People were looking to him and his mind was a total blank. Carefully controlling his voice, he said, "I would like to begin with prayer. The Bible tells us that 'if we lack wisdom, let us ask of God, who gives to all men liberally, without finding fault, and it shall be given him.' We need a lot of wisdom here. Not just our ideas, but wisdom from God."

They bowed their heads, and Mr. Li began. The others followed. They poured out their hearts to God, asking for wisdom, thanking God for his love for Mona, and his desire to restore her.

After their prayer time, they turned to Mr. Li, who was silently claiming the promise that God would put into his mouth what he should speak. So Mr. Li opened his mouth and started.

17

Over the next few weeks, Mr. Li thought a lot about Mona. How could they help her? At the end of the evening she had prayed a simple prayer to receive Jesus as her Savior—the one who cared for her and wanted to restore her to wholeness. Mr. Li had carefully explained that no matter how badly we have messed up, God still wants to draw us to himself. He pointed out the various women in Jesus' life, and how he did not condemn them, but told them to change their lives and start living holy lives. Mona had accepted Christ's work on the cross for her sins, and she had prayed and made Jesus Lord of her life. The words came easily enough. Following through with her life was going to be a real struggle.

Before they left, Mr. Li asked Mona for a list of the names of her family members who were giving her the hardest time. Each of them took this list and promised to pray for these people daily, so that Mona could have some release from their bitter attitudes.

The following day, Mr. Li took a trip across the city on public transport. The small van he entered was full of people. He paid his fare to the driver, who was busy on his cell phone. During the course of her trip, Mr. Li observed the driver as he talked first on the phone and then to the passengers in the van. Mr. Li overheard that someone near to the driver was in the hospital and needed money for an operation. The driver, along with other members of the tribe elsewhere, were on their phones trying to raise the funds that were needed. During the entire journey, this man telephoned his friends and acquaintances to ask them to pledge help. He collected a few dollars here and there from his passengers. In between, he would call back to the hospital to report his progress.

Everyone was given the opportunity to participate in this community action, even the passengers, and people responded. Everyone seemed to understand that if a lot of people gave a little, then the total could be reached, so people gladly dug into their pockets to help this stranger. Those who were closer to the situation gave more, but everyone felt good about working together, in the spirit of community. Even Mr. Li reached into his pocket to get some money. To his surprise, he only had a large denomination bill. He gulped and was about to put it back, but everyone was doing their part. So, he passed it to the driver.

The driver looked down at the bill, and then with a surprised look, his eyes met Mr. Li's. "May God bless your hand," he said to Mr. Li. Then he excitedly called his friends at the hospital about how much money he had raised. Everyone in the taxi was in good spirits. One of the passengers insisted he stop for a minute so he could ask a storekeeper, who was close to him, for a donation. He returned a few minutes later with some money and passed it to the driver. Mr. Li was very thoughtful as they drove along. He was very impressed with how people cared for each other, and were helpful, even to strangers.

The following day, Mr. and Mrs. Smith drove David to the hospital in their automobile. They met Mr. Li at a nearby café.

"I've been thinking about Mona," David began. "Perhaps we should help her by renting her an apartment. That way, she will get out from her family."

"Yes," Mrs. Smith agreed. "I've wondered about the same thing."

Mr. Li let them talk for a few minutes, and then he interrupted. "I don't think it is a good idea," he said. "Single women don't live in their own apartments. If they did, they would be thought of as immoral girls with no family to protect them. If Mona had her own apartment and no visible means of income, her family would be very upset. They might even kill her."

"You're right," Mr. Smith said quietly. "She cannot live by herself." He paused. "How about we ask Anna if she could move in with her and her roommate?"

"It is a possibility," Mr. Li continued, "but I wonder what Mona's family would think. They might still think bad things. After all, it would be single girls living together."

"What should we do?"

"I think we should support her while she lives with her family. They are her family. They need to take care of her."

"But what about her future?"

Mr. Li smiled. "We can pray that God provides her with a husband. This would be the best solution. A Christian husband—we need to ask for that."

"You're right," Mrs. Smith answered. "But those things seem so hard to ask for. But we need to exercise our faith and seek God for a solution."

"I think we should get some people together who can be Mona's friends," David said. "People who will love her and care for her. She should be at events where she can be a normal girl and not feel badly about herself."

"What are you thinking?" Mrs. Smith asked.

"We should have a party. A fun party. She should be part of it."

"But why would we have a party? We need an excuse to invite people."

Mr. Li suddenly looked embarrassed.

"What is it?" Mrs. Smith laughed. Everyone looked at Mr. Li.

"My birthday is on Friday."

"Perfect," Mrs. Smith laughed. "Let's have a birthday party at our house. Mr. Li, you invite your friends. We will prepare a party and make sure that Mona is there. I will call you when we have arranged with Mona what time she can come."

Several nights later, a crowd gathered at the Smith's house. Several carloads of people came from the hospital. Ahmed and the cleaners were there. Zay'id came, as did a number of others. Mrs. Smith had invited several other foreign couples. They were strangers to Mr. Li, but they had met Mona. So, Mr. Li was happy that they were attending 'his' birthday party. Mrs. Smith had made a cake. Anna and Mona served everyone tea. There was lots of laughter, storytelling, and joking. It was a good evening, and after several hours, they piled back into taxi's heading for home.

Back in his room, Mr. Li was preparing for bed when Zay'id came to the door.

"Mr. Li," he asked. "Can I ask you something in private? I don't want anyone else knowing that I asked this."

"Sure," Mr. Li smiled. "Whatever you say will stay between you and me."

"Can you tell me about Mona? She is a very attractive girl. Who are her family?"

Mr. Li smiled. He thought to himself *"I can tell you a lot about Mona, but I won't. Not yet. Not unless you are really interested."* Aloud he said something different. He told Zay'id that Mona came from a good family, and he made Zay'id promise not to tell, she also was a follower of Jesus. Zay'id nodded and didn't seem surprised at all.

"She is a new believer," Mr. Li cautioned. "She is very immature in the faith. But she does believe. She also has had a hard time. A young man asked for her, and just before the wedding broke the engagement. No one has asked for her since, and she is very concerned about her situation."

After Zay'id left, Mr. Li spent a long time lifting the whole situation up to God. He prayed that if God was in this, then the whole thing should move ahead. If not, that God would take Mona out of Zay'id thoughts.

18

Over the following weeks, there were several occasions when the group could meet. Once they went on a picnic, and several times they gathered at someone's house. Zay'id had now become a member of their small group, and even led in a short Bible study. Mr. Li was pleased with how he was progressing in his Christian life. He was also watching the slowly growing relationship between Zay'id and Mona. He was pleased that Zay'id was progressing very slowly and cautiously. He was also happy to see that Mona was now much more relaxed and confident. Her family, however, were still actively looking for a young man to marry her.

One evening, Zay'id came by Mr. Li's room to talk to him about Mona. He had been praying about it and he felt that she was the one for him. He asked Mr. Li how he should proceed, since his family did not know her family. There would be lots of questions. How did they know one another? Why was he picking this girl? Also, he was from a poorer family and might not have the money.

Mr. Li asked Zay'id to sit down, and then he closed the door. "Zay'id," he said somberly, "there is something about Mona that I need to tell you." After he had finished, Zay'id sat for a few minutes looking dazed.

"I need to pray about this more," he said softly.

"Please don't tell others about her," Mr. Li cautioned. "She is one of us now, and we need to protect her."

Two days later, Zay'id met Mr. Li at the hospital cafeteria. "I've been thinking about Mona," he said. "I still want to marry her."

Mr. Li nodded. He was happy to hear this, but he was aware of the problems. "How will you explain to your family that you know about her?"

"You are the common link," Zay'id said. "You know my father well. He respects you. You pointed her out to me. You met her at the Smith's house. You thought we might be a good match."

"Now you are going to get me into trouble," Mr. Li protested, laughter filling his eyes.

"It's true, isn't it?"

"I didn't recommend her to you, but I will now. We've seen her grow and mature in the Lord. And she is becoming a strong believer. I can't think of anyone better for you."

"Will you come with me to talk to my father?"

Several weeks later, Mona and Zay'id were married. Zay'id's family wondered why the bride price was so cheap, but everyone said that it was Mr. Li's clever negotiations. It was a Muslim wedding, since both families were Muslims and unaware that the couple were both Christians. Afterward, they moved into a small apartment near the hospital, close to Zay'id's work. Mr. Li was very pleased, as this provided them with a home near to the hospital where they could hold Bible studies. Mona was especially pleased with the idea of reaching out to others.

"God has been faithful to me; he has forgiven me and has lifted me up, restoring my honor. I want to be available to help others," she told the small group one night. Zay'id supported her in this. So, a regular Bible study began in their home, and they sought for others to join them.

Zay'id and Mona hosted a regular Bible study with David, Anna, and Mr. Li. The Smiths occasionally dropped in a well. They kept a list of prayer requests on a paper, and each week would review it, crossing off the ones God had answered, and adding others. After several weeks, the discussion in their Bible study focused on encouraging Christians to meet and fellowship with one another. "I think we should do a study on Christian community," Zay'id said. "I really don't understand the church. Is it just meetings, or is there more?"

"What do you mean?" David asked.

"Well, we meet here for Bible Study. This is nice, and we pray during the week, but there has to be more to it than just a meeting or two a week. Shouldn't we be doing more?"

"There is more," David said. "In my church, we have music and worship. We also take up a collection of money and use it for church needs or to help the poor."

"This is good," Zay'id said. "Is there more?"

"We have classes early on Sunday Morning for children and adults. Then a worship service where there is music, worship, a collection, announcements, and then a sermon."

"So that is what church is all about?" Zay'id asked. "It's a meeting once or twice a week?"

"No, it's more than that. We have women's meetings, men's meetings, youth meetings, minister's meetings, and so on."

"It sounds like a lot of meetings. Isn't there something else to Christianity?" Zay'id sounded disappointed. "Muslims pray five times a day. They have pilgrimages and a whole month of fasting."

"We also have some special holidays, like Christmas and Easter," David said defensively.

"I think your idea is a good idea," Mr. Li interjected. "Why don't we study what it means to be a church?"

"Okay," David said. "Who is going to lead us?"

"Well, what does the Bible teach us about churches?"

"I don't know. It's probably a complicated subject."

"Well," said Mr. Li. "I'm thinking of four names that the Bible gives to the church. Perhaps we could start there."

"What are the four names?"

"What do you think, David?"

"Well, there is 'church.'"

"Yes, that is the meeting of believers. We can study that one. Is there another?"

"How about the 'kingdom?'" Anna asked. "Aren't Christians referred to as a kingdom?"

"Yes, that is a good one. We can study that as well."

"Aren't we also called the Body of Christ?" Zay'id asked.

"Very good, I think there is one more," Mr. Li encouraged them.

Mona looked shy. "I remember reading something about the bride of Christ."

"I wonder why you remember that one," Zay'id joked, poking her. Mona poked back. "It just caught my attention one day."

"Well," said Mr. Li, "those four will make good topics for four Bible studies. Who want to take a subject and prepare it?"

19

In the months following Mona and Zay'id's marriage, Mona's sister Asma quietly observed what was happening in their marriage and home. From the beginning, she had not believed that Mona would ever be happily married. Part of this stemmed from her own unhappy marriage, and part of it stemmed from the fact that she also had also been abused by her brother, but no pregnancy had ever resulted. She was pleased when Mona married Zay'id, for this would forever erase the possibility of shame that either of them could bring onto the family through their earlier actions. However, now that Mona was married, it seemed to her that Mona was happier than she was.

Asma's husband, Jamal, was the darling of the family when they married. He was handsome, with a wonderful smile. He seemed easy going, and she was very happy with all of the attention that she received throughout the marriage event. However, they eventually settled down in a small apartment, and she spent her days looking after their two young daughters, taking them to her parents, and living much as she used to. Except that she was now married. But Jamal was never home. He would rise before the sun came up and drive away in his taxi. He worked all day, driving around the city looking for fares. It would usually be closer to midnight when he returned. Some days he did not return, as he was on the far side of the city. He would sleep in the home of another driver, and she wouldn't see him until he came home exhausted at the end of the long day. Sometimes she wondered where all the money went that Jamal earned. Sometimes she wondered if there wasn't another woman.

Mona, on the other hand, seemed to be very happy, and perfectly fulfilled. Asma wondered how Mona had done it. How has she trapped such a pleasant young man? He had a steady job and was home every night. Their home wasn't plush, but there was something about it that was relaxing and pleasant. When Jamal was home, his rowdy friends often came over. But Mona entertained Americans and Asians. Besides that, Mona and her husband weren't very good Muslims. They didn't seem to pray, didn't attend the mosque, and she did not think that Zay'id had ever been on the pilgrimage to Mecca. They didn't have a Qur'an in their home, at least not that Asma had seen. But she had seen other religious materials. A plaque on the wall contained a saying that Asma had never heard of before. Mona had explained that it was from one of the old prophets. It was all very strange.

But then, one day, something happened that started to put things into perspective for Asma. She dropped by Mona's and found her reading in her sitting room. Mona put the book away on another table, but when she left the room, Asma moved over to see what it was. It was a Bible. Suddenly things became clearer in Asma's mind: Mona was playing around with other religions. She waited until Mona entered the room.

"What were you reading when I came in?" Asma asked innocently after the tea was poured.

"Oh, nothing much."

"It looks like such a thick book from here. Is it from a famous author?"

"Actually, there are many writers," Mona answered, and then she tried to change the subject.

"Is it a religious book?" Asma asked when it was possible to change the subject back.

"Did you look at it?"

"Yes."

"Then you know what it is."

"Yes, you were reading the Christians' book."

"I find it interesting."

"But it's been changed—corrupted."

"Yes, I've heard that, but I decided to read it myself."

"Mona," her sister looked at her sternly, "are you a Christian?"

Mona caught her breath. Was should she answer? Everything could be ruined. But how could she deny the one who had met her need? She took a deep breath. "I've found such beautiful things in the Gospels," she started. "The prophet Jesus brought such a message of hope and encouragement."

"I knew it," Asma said. "You are such a bad girl. First you get pregnant, now you are forsaking our religion."

"That's not fair," Mona protested. "You don't know my situation."

"I'm going to tell your husband," Asma said triumphantly.

Mona stopped, eyes wide. "Tell him what?"

"That you were pregnant before you were married, that you were not a virgin. He will divorce you!"

"Oh that," Mona said, "he already knows that. He knew that before we were married."

"He did?" Asma was incredulous. "I don't understand it. He still married you."

"Yes," Mona said gently. "He did it out of love. He did it to restore my honor. He did it to restore all of our honor. He is such a wonderful man, Asma. I'm so lucky that God brought him into my life."

"God? What has God got to do with this?"

"The Bible tells us that God wants to restore us and remake us into new and different people. That's why I'm reading, Asma. I'm learning all about the messages that God sent. Right from the very beginning, he has been revealing himself and his will to the world. You should read it too."

"Do you think it will help my marriage?"

"God can help your marriage, Asma. I've noticed that you haven't been very happy lately. Jamal never seems to be around. Can I pray for you and your marriage?"

Asma didn't know what to say. She hadn't thought of her sister Mona as being especially religious. Now she was offering to pray. She stared at her sister, and then a yearning started to grow in her heart for a better marriage. Slowly she nodded 'yes.'

Mona didn't wait. She immediately raised her hands in front of her, closed her eyes and began to pray: "Lord God, thank you so much for reaching out to me in my need. Thank you so much for restoring my honor and making me who I am today. Thank you so much for providing me with a loving husband. Dear God, I ask that you would bless my sister's marriage. Lord, bless Jamal, and help him to be a loving husband and father. Bless Asma, she is so dear to my heart and I love her so much. Please reach out to her and reveal yourself to her, as you have done to me."

As Mona finished praying, tears were slipping down Asma's face. Mona reached over and gently wiped them off. Then she softly kissed her sister's forehead. "Would you like to leave your children here some times? I would be happy to watch the girls if you need to go shopping or something."

Asma was so shocked. She had been thinking evil things about her sister. The love that she was being shown melted her heart.

That night Mr. Li, David, Anna, and the Smiths met at Zay'id and Mona's house for their Bible study. Their study that night was about laying up treasure in heaven, not on the earth. At the end of the study, Mona shared something with the group.

"You know, when Zay'id asked my family if they could marry me, my family were so eager to get me married that they never asked for any gold for me." Zay'id looked a bit concerned. "Gold," Mona explained to David and Anna, "is very important for the bride. It is the only thing that she will own in her married life. The house, the furniture, the children, all belong to the husband. If they ever divorce, she can only take her personal gold and what she wears with her. My family never asked for gold." She paused. "But in marrying me to Zay'id, they gave me something more precious than gold. I have a wonderful, loving, Godly man. I'm so happy." Zay'id's face was beaming.

Mona continued, "today, I was reminded of that, when my sister came to my house. She has gold, a nice apartment, two beautiful girls, and a nice husband. But she is unhappy. Today she saw the Bible in our house and asked a lot of questions about it. I loaned it to her to read. Can we pray for her? She wants us to pray that she will have as happy a marriage as I do."

"Well," said David slowly, "I think your marriage is as good as it is because Zay'id is a follower of Jesus. Perhaps we should pray that Jamal also becomes a follower of Jesus."

"That would be a good start." Mona smiled.

Asma was in tears when Mona arrived at their parent's house in the late afternoon some days later. The whole family was quickly gathering. Everyone was there, including Jamal, who looked rather sheepish. Earlier that day he had had a car accident and his taxi was badly damaged. The police said that it was his fault. His car would be in the repair shop for a week or more. That meant no income. And there were bills to pay. The family was devastated. It was a very bad time for this to happen. The other family members were also stretched financially.

"Please come by our house tonight," Mona said to Asma and Jamal when there was an opportunity to talk to them alone. "I will talk to Zay'id, and I'm sure we can help you." Jamal nodded thankfully.

A couple of hours later, Mona and Zay'id were home. It was their Bible Study night, so everyone had gathered in their living room. They were in the middle of their study when the doorbell rang. It was Asma, Jamal, and their two small daughters. Zay'id invited them in. They were a bit surprised at the group that was gathered, but sat down and accepted some tea.

"Tell us about the accident," Mona asked Jamal. So he explained what had happened and how he had not foreseen what would take place. His taxi was now badly damaged.

"Do you have a good mechanic who can fix it?" Mr. Smith asked, genuinely concerned.

"I know of some body shops, but I don't have any special connections."

"Well, maybe I can help. The man I work with, his brother, owns a body shop. We are very close friends, and I'm sure I can get you a good price. Don't go just anywhere. Just check the prices. Give me your phone number and I will arrange to bring him over to your car tomorrow so he can see it."

Jamal seemed genuinely thankful.

"So what will you do for money, now that your car is broken?" David asked.

Jamal shrugged with open hands, indicating that he didn't know.

"You have rent to pay and two little kids to feed," David continued, indicating the girls. "I would like to help you." He reached for his wallet. Anna was already reaching for her purse.

"We would all like to help," Mr. Li said with a smile. "I imagine some of us can give more, and some less, but we would all like to contribute."

Mona grabbed a red plastic pitcher from the kitchen and they passed it around. Everyone put something in. Then Mona dumped it into a plastic bag. "Here, this will help."

"I will check with you all in a couple of days," Zay'id said, "and let you know if they need any more." Jamal didn't seem to notice the Bibles around the room, but Asma recognized them. She made a point to talk more to Mona the next day.

The following day, Mona and Asma discussed what was happening in their lives. "You prayed that I would have a better marriage and that Jamal would be home more. Well, now he is home all the time. I'm scared of your prayers," Asma said with a bit of mocking in her voice.

"God answers in mysterious ways," Mona replied.

"Can you tell me more about Jesus?" Asma asked. "I've been reading about him, but I read so poorly that I have a hard time getting much."

Two weeks later, Jamal's car was fixed. Mr. Smith's contact had proven very helpful, and Mr. Smith had slipped him several hundred dollars. Jamal was shocked at the amount. "I'm always happy to help someone in need. You don't have to pay it back. Just be willing to help the next person God brings across your path, who is in need."

Jamal nodded. He then asked Mr. Smith about God. Was he a Muslim? A long conversation followed.

A few days later, Jamal made a surprising announcement to Asma. "Tomorrow I would like to visit Mona and Zay'id." He paused. "They are meeting with Mr. Li and others at their house to study the Bible. Mona didn't think you would mind."

Asma was shocked. She nodded, and then stepped close to her husband and kissed him. For some reason her heart was filled with love for him. It was a new and wonderful feeling. God was certainly doing something in their lives!

20

"But the Bible has been changed," Jamal insisted. "Everyone knows that."

Mr. Smith shook his head. "Everyone saying it doesn't make it correct. The Bible I have here was translated from very old documents."

"But the translations are not trustworthy," Jamal countered.

"In my country, many pastors learn to read Greek and Hebrew. It is part of their training so that they can read the documents in their original language."

"But those documents are not trustworthy."

"I wonder," Mr. Smith said slowly, "Can you tell me when the Bible was changed? Was it before or after the prophet Muhammad?"

"I guess it was after Muhammad," Jamal said thoughtfully. "He refers to the 'people of the book' in a positive way."

"The Bible I am holding here is translated from documents that are much earlier. The Old Testament, the writings of the prophets, come from documents that pre-date Muhammad by more than six hundred years. And every time archeologists dig up old copies, they are the same as what I am holding here."

Jamal scowled.

"Besides," Mr. Smith said gently, "imagine the problem that one would have trying to change the Bible. The Jewish people had the Torah for many centuries. There were thousands of copies in homes, synagogues, and schools. The only way someone could have changed the Bible is to have destroyed all of the old ones; not only them, but everything written about them. It would mean a massive destruction of all Jewish religious literature. Otherwise, we would have conflicting copies today. But we don't."

Jamal didn't look convinced. He tried another argument. "You Christians say that God had a son. I cannot believe this. God never took a wife and had a son. God does not beget nor is begotten. Jesus is just another of the prophets."

Mr. Smith smiled at Jamal, trying to put him at ease. "Jamal," he began, "who is like Jesus? Think about him for a moment. He was sinless, he did many miracles and healings. He demonstrated his power over nature. At his birth, angels appeared. The stars moved. All of these things demonstrate that God was plainly indicating to us that this was no ordinary man, nor an ordinary prophet. He is special." He paused for a moment to think. "Tell me, who is coming again? Are any of the prophets coming again? No, only Jesus is coming again. This is God's mark on him that he is different from the prophets."

Jamal fidgeted a bit. He didn't look convinced.

"Look," Mr. Smith continued, "no Christian anywhere believes that God had sex with a woman and produced a son. This is blasphemy. It is blasphemy for you and for us. Please don't even think it! Also..." Mr. Smith paused. "Christians are not trying to make a man into God. We are proclaiming that God became a man. He was made in our image so that we and he could communicate to us. And more than this, so that our sins could be dealt with and removed."

"I still don't think he was the 'Son of God,'" Jamal protested.

"Look at Luke 1: 30-33" Mr. Smith countered. "The angel appears to Mary and says 'do not be afraid, Mary, you have found favor with God. You will be with child and give birth to a son, and you are to give him the name Jesus. He will be great and will be called the Son of the Most High. The Lord God will give him the throne of his father David, and he will reign over the house of Jacob forever; his kingdom will never end.' This is the angel Gabriel speaking. Are you going to argue with Gabriel?"

Jamal looked defeated.

"Let's look at Luke 3:23," Mr. Smith said with genuine concern in his voice. "'A voice came from heaven, which said, Thou art my beloved Son; in thee I am well pleased.' This is God speaking directly from heaven. Are you going to argue with God?"

Jamal was quiet as Mr. Smith went on to outline what it was that Christians believed, and how Jesus' death on the cross provided an answer for the problem of sin. Jamal and Asma both listened very closely.

As it was growing late, Mona interrupted and suggested that they meet again at her home. So, they arranged to meet again in two days' time. As Asma and Jamal left with their two girls, Asma reflected on how happy she had been the last couple of days. She was now enjoying a renewed relationship with her sister Mona; she was spending some evenings with Jamal, and many of her questions about Christians were being answered.

Mr. and Mrs. Smith were excited about their meeting with Jamal and Asma. They arrived early so that they would have time to pray and prepare themselves.

"That was so exciting," Mrs. Smith exclaimed. "They seem so keen. I think they are very close to accepting Christ."

"Yes," Mr. Smith agreed. "Let's pray that this is the night they accept Jesus as their Savior."

After a short prayer time, Jamal and Asma arrived. Jamal was full of smiles, and they started with lots of jokes. Jamal described visiting the shop that was fixing his taxi. He was very happy with the work being done. The group talked about some of the things that were on the TV news that night. Asma and Mona were talking about shopping for children's clothing. Meanwhile, Mr. and Mrs. Smith were getting anxious. The evening was slowly moving on and they had not yet spoken of spiritual things.

David arrived late and apologized. There had been a big car accident, and the highway was closed. He described the scene as he had witnessed it, as his taxi slowly made its way past the three wrecked cars. Jamal then added several stories about car accidents that he had seen during his days driving a taxi. Then Zay'id and Jamal got into an animated discussion about car insurance, and how poor the companies were at paying out after an accident. They then asked Mr. Smith about his insurance and what insurance cost in America.

Mr. Smith cleared his throat, wondering how to answer and then quickly change the subject to something spiritual. But how does one move from car insurance to the gospel? He didn't have to worry too long. David jumped into the conversation and answered the question about insurance. Mr. Smith groaned inside and looked helplessly at his wife. She rolled her eyes and looked the other way. Both of them were frustrated.

After endless cups of tea and coffee, biscuits and sweets, the evening started to wind down. As everyone stood to leave, Asma and Jamal thanked everyone for a wonderful visit. Asma was especially pleased. This was the first time she had seen Jamal so relaxed and enjoying himself. She had enjoyed the evening very much and felt that it had been a great boost to their marriage relationship. She was so happy that they had friends that they could be open and free with. She felt very close to this group. That night Jamal held her hand in the taxi during their ride home. Asma was almost in tears as they arrived home. She whisked the girls to their beds so that Jamal wouldn't see how wet her eyes were, not with sadness but with joy.

The Smiths, on the other hand, were very frustrated.

"That was a real waste of time," Mr. Smith fumed as they drove home. "I'm really surprised that David derailed the conversation so many times."

"Yes," Mrs. Smith agreed. "We got nowhere tonight. There wasn't a single spiritual conversation in the whole evening. I'm sure sorry that Mr. Li couldn't have been there. He might have been able to salvage things."

"I sure hope that the next time we meet we can discuss spiritual things. I thought they were so close, and then this."

That night, Mr. and Mrs. Smith barely talked to each other. They were both very disappointed. After a short prayer together, they went to sleep.

21

Several days later, the Smiths, Mona and Zay'id and Asma and Jamal met again. Anna was also there but offered to take the girls into another room to play with them.

"Well," Mr. Smith smiled, making sure he could direct the conversation from the first. "We started talking the other day about Christian things. Do you have questions about Christianity that you want to discuss?"

"Actually, Asma and I have been talking about the things you have been sharing with us, and we were wondering if you all wouldn't mind answering a few more of our questions."

"Sure," Mr. Smith smiled, "we can try, but there is no guarantee that we have all the answers. But we will try."

"We were wondering about how Christians pray."

"I don't understand."

"Well, we were wondering if we could visit a church and observe what people are doing."

"Well, I can tell you about it," Mr. Smith started. "It's really pretty simple. We sing some songs, read the Bible, pray, and someone preaches a sermon."

"We would really like to visit a church to see this."

"I don't know." Mr. Smith looked confused. "The church that my wife and I attend is in English. It is on the other side of town."

"Do men and women pray together?" Asma asked. "In Islam, only the men enter the mosque, unless there is a special room for women."

"Yes, we mix together. Men and women sit together."

"You sit when you pray? Do you sit on the floor like in a mosque?"

"No, we sit on chairs."

"Chairs? Do you sit through the whole prayer time?"

"Actually, sometimes we sit and sometimes we stand."

"Do you bow down?"

"No, we don't bow down. We either sit or stand."

"And men and women sit together?"

"Yes."

"So, do some men sometimes sit by another man's wife?"

"Yes, but I don't understand where this is leading. We just come and sit and worship," Mr. Smith said, slightly exasperated.

"What do you mean by worship?"

"That includes singing, praying, and studying God's word." Mrs. Smith offered.

"Don't forget the offering," Mr. Smith added. "That is also part of our worship. We worship God with our tithes and offerings."

"To whom do you give your money?"

"We pass a plate around, actually more like a large bowl, and people put their money in it."

"You must pass it through the crowd?"

"Yes, sort of."

"Does anyone needy ever take money out?"

"No, we just pass it around. We have men called 'ushers' who pass the plate and people place the money in it."

"Who gets the money?"

"Well, the ushers count it, and it is given to the leaders of the church to decide what to do with it."

"Do ushers ever steal money?"

"We hope not," Mr. Smith joked. "Usually we have two or three men there when the money is counted."

"You don't trust one another?"

Mr. Smith was getting annoyed. "Don't you have any more questions about Jesus?"

"Actually, we were wondering about fasting. Do Christians fast?"

At the end of the meeting, Mr. Smith was quite upset, but he managed to smile and say goodbye to everyone. A few days later he met with Mr. Li and David.

"I don't know why we are messing around with Asma and Jamal. I don't really think they are interested in the gospel."

"Why do you say that?" Mr. Li asked.

"Because their questions are all about how we pray, how we hold our hands when we worship, who counts the offering money, do we fast like Muslims in the month of Ramada, and, get this," Mr. Smith snorted, "Jamal wanted to know if we went to Jerusalem or Bethlehem for our pilgrimage."

"Didn't you talk about Jesus or God?" David asked.

"No, nothing like that. All he wanted to talk about was comparing religious forms. Did we stand or sit, and when? It was all very strange."

Mr. Li had been quiet up until this time. "Perhaps they really want to know more about Christianity, and this is their way of doing it."

"I don't know." Mr. Smith said. "It sure seems strange to me. I want to talk about God and explain about Jesus' death on the cross: theology, not religion."

"Perhaps they have never talked about theology," Mr. Li said. "Perhaps his experience with Islam has been all about doing religion. He may not know anything else."

Mr. Smith looked at Mr. Li. "That's very interesting. Very interesting. I'm going to have to think about this. I'm ready to argue theology. I really don't know how to do anything else."

Mr. Smith was excited. Jamal had called him and told him he would like to meet for lunch so they could talk, just the two of them. *Now we are going to get somewhere,* Mr. Smith thought. He asked his wife to pray, and he drove to the small restaurant that Jamal had suggested. As he entered, he realized that he had not been to this kind of place before. The main floor was filled with tables of noisy men in rough working clothes. There were no women there. Then he noticed a balcony overlooking the restaurant. Jamal was waving for him from one of the tables that overlooked the main seating area. Mr. Smith made his way up the stairs and over to the small table where Jamal was seated.

"I'm very glad to see you," Jamal smiled.

"Thank you for inviting me. This looks like a very interesting place."

"Really?" Jamal looked puzzled. "It's just one restaurant like many others." The waiter approached them. "I'll have a small one," Jamal said, "and he will have a large one." He indicated Mr. Smith, who has a little overweight.

"What would you like to drink?" the waiter asked.

"What you would like?" Jamal asked.

"What do they have?"

"Pepsi, water, tea," Jamal said, looking a bit lost.

"I'll have a Pepsi," Mr. Smith said, thinking of all the germs he might pick up in a place like this. Pepsi was at least sanitary. Jamal ordered the same.

"You have a nice view out of this open window," Mr. Smith commented, looking out onto the street below, "and a nice view of the restaurant downstairs."

"I like this place," Jamal answered. "I often come here to eat lunch—when I'm driving my taxi, of course." He was interrupted by the waiter who brought them a basket of flat bread and a dish of humus dip with lots of olive oil. Jamal passed Mr. Smith a piece of bread and ripped a piece off of his own. He dipped it into the humus and began to eat. Mr. Smith had done this before, and he followed suit.

After they had eaten the humus, the waiter arrived with two plates, one for each of them. Jamal's was a smaller dish of rice, and Mr. Smith's was a larger dish. Then the waiter brought a dish of meat and green beans in a thick sauce. Jamal offered the meat dish to Mr. Smith first and then he took some over his rice. They ate with a spoon.

A few minutes later, the air was filled with a blast of sound. Mr. Smith suddenly realized that a mosque was located right outside the window, across the street. A loudspeaker was aimed right at their table. As the mullah gave the call for prayer, the dishes on their table rattled from the impact of the noise.

"Stupid mosque," Jamal muttered. "It's too loud." Mr. Smith was startled by this outburst against Islam. "Why are they permitted to make so much noise?" Jamal continued. "The prayer call is a bother. Islam is a false religion, anyway."

Mr. Smith was surprised by these comments. Jamal continued: "Muslims are such donkeys. Those mullahs are just blind people leading the blind. They should be all shut up. Don't you agree?"

Mr. Smith didn't know how to respond. Silently, he prayed and called out to God for help. He had never been in this situation before. "Help me say the right thing," he silently prayed. Then he opened his mouth and spoke. "My book, the Bible, teaches us to speak respectfully of all men, even when we disagree with them. Disrespect is a sin that God will judge us on." Jamal grew quiet. "We must pray for them, not be angry with them. There was a time when I too was far from God. God had to draw me to himself." He paused and took some food and then a drink. Jamal nodded and then changed the topic. The rest of the conversation was about other topics. At the end of the meal, Jamal paid, and Mr. Smith drove home.

"It was a very strange visit," he told his wife later. "I thought it was a total waste of time. We didn't talk about anything much. But at the end of the visit, Jamal asked if he and Asma could come and visit us tonight."

"Tonight?" Mrs. Smith protested. "But I was planning on shopping tonight. There are lots of things we need."

"I told them we would be home by 7:00."

"Oh no, what will I serve them?"

"We still have time to go out and get something, and perhaps get some shopping done," Mr. Smith tried to console his wife as they rushed out the door.

A bit after 7:00 pm, Jamal and Asma arrived at the Smith's door. They explained that they had left their children with Zay'id and Mona. "It will do them good," Jamal teased, "they need the practice."

After they had sat down around a cup of tea and fancy sweets that Mrs. Smith had purchased, Jamal got right to the point. "We are interested in becoming Christians."

Mr. Smith was shocked. Mrs. Smith almost dropped her cup of tea.

Jamal looked puzzled. "What do we have to do to become Christians?"

"Well," Mr. Smith responded slowly. "You must believe in your heart that Jesus died on the cross for your sins, and you must confess him with your mouth."

"Asma and I have been reading the Bible, and, yes, we do believe that he died on the cross. But how do we confess him?"

"Well," Mr. Smith looked startled. "In my country, you need to pray the sinner's prayer."

"What is that?"

"Well, I start and you follow me. Just repeat after me what I say."

"Okay." Jamal seemed totally willing to do whatever the Smiths instructed. So, Mr. and Mrs. Smith bowed their heads. "Dear Lord Jesus" Mr. Smith began.

"Dear Lord Jesus," Jamal and Asma repeated together.

"Thank you for dying on the cross in my place."

"Thank you for dying on the cross in my place," they repeated.

"Thank you for forgiving my sins."

"Thank you for forgiving my sins," they repeated.

"Thank you for making me your child."

"Thank you for making me your child."

"Amen."

"Amen."

Mr. Smith realized that he wasn't doing a very good job of this, but he had been so surprised that he wasn't thinking very clearly.

When they looked up, Mrs. Smith was crying. Jamal and Asma smiled shyly. Mr. Smith gave Jamal a big hug, while Mrs. Smith hugged Asma. They drank some more tea and Mr. Smith suggested they begin to meet for weekly discipleship lessons. Jamal was happy with it, and they agreed to meet every Tuesday evening.

After Jamal and Asma left, Mr. Smith grabbed his wife and danced around her. "I'm so excited," he almost shouted. "I just led my first Muslim to Christ!"

Mrs. Smith was excited too. "Just wait until we tell Zay'id and Mona." They finally settled down and wrote out a list of topics that they would cover in their weekly discipleship times. Surprisingly, Zay'id and Mona were not as excited as the Smiths. They did smile and responded to the Smiths enthusiasm, but they expressed doubts that Jamal and Asma had really accepted Christ.

22

Jamal and Asma were quickly growing in the faith. Jamal was back driving his taxi, but he was also regularly reading his Bible and listening to Christian music in his car. Asma was also faithfully reading. Besides this, whenever she visited with Mona, they almost always had a spiritual discussion. Often Mona didn't know how to answer her sister's questions, so they would note them for their next meeting with Mr. Li or the Smiths.

Several weeks had passed when the group decided to go on a picnic together. They planned to leave on Friday morning, since everyone had the day off. Jamal, Zay'id, and Mr. Smith had cars. Zay'id brought along a small metal box to use as a barbeque. The ladies brought meat, vegetables and salads. The Smiths brought along cookies and several cases of Pepsi. Mr. Li and Ahmed brought fruit. David brought bread, and Anna brought sweet pastries.

Jamal led them to a deserted hillside outside of the city. They pulled off the road into a rocky area. They parked the cars near some scraggly trees and carried everything up into a thicker grove of scraggly trees. As they were putting down a mat and setting up, Anna took Jamal's girls exploring. Soon everyone was sitting around on the ground. Ahmed and Zay'id started a small fire. They soon placed a teapot onto the hot coals.

It was a very relaxed day. They spent several hours talking and visiting. Mr. Smith enjoyed the first hour of the visiting, but speaking and thinking in the local language was hard work, and he soon grew tired, and dropped out of the conversation. Being a very busy man, he found himself becoming impatient. He could be at home doing several important things, and here he was, sitting under a tree, wasting his time. But he stayed because he felt it was the right thing to do. The men talked and joked, sitting in a small circle around the fire. The women sat off to the side and spoke together, but Mr. Smith really couldn't hear them. It seemed like hours before someone suggested that they start cooking the food. Then the barbeque was set up and Zay'id started the process of making hot coals. It was a long time before the meat was cooking. Eventually, everyone was happily eating meat wrapped in flat bread.

After the meal, the girls went to sleep on a blanket, and the men continued to visit. Mr. Smith was getting desperate to leave, but he didn't know how to excuse himself without disappointing the others.

It was late afternoon when the men started discussing what they enjoyed about the group. To Mr. Smith, it was just another discussion topic, but Mr. Li sensed that the conversation was moving toward spiritual things.

"I really enjoy the fellowship," Zay'id commented. "My family is great, but with this group, I feel much more at home."

"I enjoy Mr. Smith's cookies," Jamal said, smiling.

"Not my pastries?" Anna teased.

"The pastries are good." Jamal was quick to correct himself. "But the cookies are my favorite."

"Maybe you should have married an American wife," Asma teased him, poking him in the ribs.

"I can teach you how to make cookies," Mrs. Smith offered with a smile.

"Yes," Jamal quickly agreed. "Please teach her how to make cookies—especially this kind."

"The cookies are good," Zay'id said with a sly grin, "but the best thing I like about this group is that this is where I met my wife."

"That's even better than cookies," Jamal joked. "It worked for you, but David here is still single. Well, there is another single girl here,"

Jamal joked again. When Anna turned red with embarrassment, he quickly changed the subject. "When Asma first talked about this group, I thought it sounded pretty strange. Asma was happy about attending, so I let her go, but I wasn't really interested. It wasn't until God took my taxi from me in the accident that I came to realize how wonderful this group is. Everyone offered to help me in some way. I was so amazed. Usually only family helps this way, and my family wasn't offering to do very much."

"Now you know where your real family is," Mrs. Smith interjected. "We are part of the family of God, and that makes us all brothers and sisters."

"Yes," Jamal said slowly, "that is correct, but I wasn't part of this family. I didn't know anything. I was even against you. But you guys all helped me." He paused. "I was totally amazed that you would help me, a stranger. And you didn't ask for anything back."

Everyone was silent, listening.

"I argued with Mr. Smith about things. You know, the Bible being changed and all. And he had good answers for me. But that wasn't enough. After several weeks, I was convinced that Jesus was God's sacrifice for sins. Asma and I talked it over many times. But I still wasn't sure if these Americans were not out to destroy Islam. I thought that they might be just pro-America and wanting to destroy my religion."

He paused and looked at Mr. Smith. "That's when I decided to test Mr. Smith." Several eyebrows were raised. "I invited him to a restaurant beside a mosque, right when the call to prayer would happen. I then complained about Islam to see if he would join me. He refused and said that we should honor and respect everyone. It was then that I realized that Mr. Smith was different from all my Muslim friends. God had truly changed his heart. I wanted to be like that."

Mr. Smith was shocked. He tried to smile and say something nice, but inside he was reeling. He had not realized that Jamal was testing him. What would have happened if he had complained about the call to prayer? He certainly had felt like complaining, but God had restrained him. If he had complained, would Jamal not have accepted Christ?

"I guess I saw something in each of you that I recognized as similar. I wanted to have the same and be part of you guys."

"So it wasn't all about theology?" Mr. Smith asked softly.

"Theology? No, I was attracted to who you all were."

"I don't know about the others," Mr. Li said softly. "There isn't much in me that is attractive. If you see anything attractive, you must be seeing Christ in me."

"It wasn't so much what I saw in one person," Jamal said thoughtfully. "It was that I was seeing the same thing in all of you. You were all different. You all had different personalities. And yet, there was that something in your life that I wanted. It wasn't until I understood that it was Jesus, that I also wanted to become a Christian."

"That doesn't sound like very good theology," Mr. Smith commented. "You became a Christian, so that you could be like us, not because of what Jesus did for you."

"Well, yes and no," Jamal protested. "I don't know much about the Jesus that lived two thousand years ago, but I do know about what I saw in each of you. Once I recognized it as Jesus, I wanted it." He paused. "And now I am starting to understand about sin and Jesus' death on the cross for sin."

"And," Zay'id said slyly, "you are becoming like us, just like you wanted. Look, you already like cookies so much that you want your wife to start making them."

"Cookies are great," Jamal joked. "I wonder if the apostle Paul liked cookies."

Several weeks after the picnic, the Smiths were visiting Zay'id and Mona when Jamal and Asma dropped in for a visit.

"Remember that picnic?" Jamal asked. "That was a great day. I will never forget it."

"*I won't either,*" Mr. Smith thought to himself. "*It was such a long day, and I failed to accomplish anything useful that day. All we did was sit around, drink tea and talk.*" But aloud he said, "it was a good picnic. I recall that you liked my wife's cookies."

"I'm learning to make them." Asma smiled. "I've made them once with your wife, and soon I will try them by myself."

"It wasn't just the cookies," Jamal said. "I enjoyed being around good people. There were no bad stories and wrong thoughts."

"I suppose you get those when driving the taxi," Mrs. Smith joked.

"Actually I used to get lots of questions about where to pick up girls," Jamal answered. Asma was watching him closely. "But now that I play Christian songs, people don't ask those sorts of questions." He paused. "The bad stories usually came from other taxi drivers. I don't know if I would believe half of them."

"Yes," Zay'id said. "I'm enjoying being with the group more than with my family. I'm really much more relaxed, and don't feel I have to always put on a good front. I can just be me."

"I wonder," Jamal said thoughtfully, "can I invite some of my friends? I think they would enjoy it too."

"Yes," Zay'id said. "We usually are just the few of us. I was wondering about inviting my friends."

"To a Bible study?" Mrs. Smith asked incredulously. "If they are Muslims, won't they be offended?"

"Oh, I wouldn't bring any Muslim fanatics. But I've been talking to some of my friends and they want to see how we study and who we are."

"Well," Mr. Smith said slowly, "usually we are all Christians. I suppose we could put on a special meeting for those who are interested, a sort of seeker's meeting."

"What is that?" Jamal asked.

"It's a special meeting we put on to appeal to seekers. We do things especially to appeal to them."

"We could do that," Zay'id replied, remembering Mr. Li's birthday party where he had first met Mona. "We could host it here. Why don't we have a party and invite those we know are interested? I've talked to people; Jamal and Asma have talked to people. In fact, I'm sure we all have people we might want to invite."

"That's a good idea," said Mr. Smith. "Let's have a party and meet those in each other's lives."

"But when do we invite them to a Bible Study?" Mrs. Smith asked, thinking of her neighbor lady with whom she had been having conversations.

"Why don't we get together after the party, at our next Bible study, and decide who we should invite to the Bible study? That would give us a reason to get to know everyone," Asma answered. "I don't want a lot of strangers asking awkward questions at our Bible study. But I do want to invite a friend of mine. I think she is ready."

"Okay," Mr. Smith said. "Let's get this straight. First, we witness to our friends and neighbors. When they get interested in meeting others, we throw a party."

"Yes," Zay'id said excitedly. "Then we can meet each other's friends and get to know them. After the party we meet and decide who we should invite to our Bible Studies."

"I've been thinking of something else," Mrs. Smith said shyly. "I've been wondering if we shouldn't have a breaking of bread service."

"What is that?"

"That is when we have the Lord's Supper. I've really missed not breaking bread. I find it so meaningful."

"I think that is a great idea honey," Mr. Smith smiled. "Let's have a breaking of bread service at our next study. It might go hand in hand with our study topic."

"What's that?" Jamal asked.

"Baptism," Mr. Smith said with a smile, hoping not to shock or offend anyone.

"Oh good," Mona said under her breath. "Maybe you can answer some of my questions."

"I don't know if I can," Mr. Smith said tenderly. "But we can look at what the Bible teaches."

"I'm excited about the party," Zay'id said. "I've been wondering how I can introduce a friend of mine to this group."

23

Everyone started arriving on Friday. Zay'id and Mona were hosting the party. Anna arrived at their home early in the morning to help with the children. Asma showed up to help with cleaning and then cooking. By 6:00 pm the Smiths had arrived and food was placed on tables. By 7:00 the others started arriving.

David came right at 7:00 with his young friend, Haytham, who appeared to be very shy at first. Obviously, he felt quite out of place, but he soon warmed as the other men arrived and the visiting began. Jamal brought his friend Kamal, another taxi driver. They had been having lunches together and would often talk of spiritual things. Mr. Smith had a friend, Assaf, a shopkeeper that he had been visiting. Assaf was already reading the Bible and had many questions, not just about spiritual things, but about Christians and how they acted and behaved themselves. Assaf was especially interested in this party to see how Christians behaved themselves. He was pleased to note that the women met in the living room and that the men were seated on plastic chairs on the cement rooftop.

Down in the living room, there were several new female faces as well. Maysoon and Gada were Mona's friends from the same apartment building. They came for a few minutes and then left as they had families that didn't know about the party. They told their families that they were visiting each other and then raced downstairs to be at Mona's party for a few minutes. They were especially interested in meeting Mrs. Smith and Anna. A new girl, Nadia, was there with her husband, Afif. Asma and Jamal had invited them. Nadia had been talking a lot to Asma, but Afif was unfamiliar with most spiritual things.

Mr. Li and Dr. Wilson arrived a bit later with Ahmed and another middle-aged man, Abdullah. Most of the evening was spent just visiting and talking about life in general. Several times, spiritual conversations were started. Afif seemed lost during these conversations, but Kamal and Assaf were eager to talk.

Conversation turned to religion quite quickly. Afif was intrigued by Mr. Li. He thought that most Chinese were Muslims or atheists and was surprised to discover that Mr. Li was a Christian. Soon, he and Mr. Li were comparing religions. Afif was convinced that Islam was superior to Christianity.

"Our leader was a great leader. He ruled a kingdom, commanded armies, had men and women at his command, married many wives, and heard the voice of God. He founded the greatest religion in the world. Jesus was a failure. He only preached for a couple of years, and then he was gone. His followers are divided. He never even married."

Mr. Li smiled. "I agree with you. Compared to Muhammad, Jesus wasn't a very successful ruler. Mohammad began a great empire." He paused. "Do you know what Jesus said about his kingdom?"

Afif looked puzzled. "No, what did he say?"

Mr. Li took out a New Testament. "Here in the gospel of John, chapter 18, Jesus says 'My kingdom is not of this world. If it were, my servants would fight to prevent my arrest by the Jews. But now my kingdom is from another place.' What do you think he meant by this?"

"I have no idea." Several of the other men had stopped talking to listen.

"Muhammad, and those that came after him, focused on a great earthly kingdom, and in this they were successful. They built an empire from Spain to Indonesia." Afif was nodding. "Jesus was focusing on another kingdom. One that was not of this world. In other words, it was somewhere else. Listen to what he says in John 14: 'Do not let your hearts be troubled. Trust in God; trust also in me. In my Father's house are many rooms; if it were not so, I would have told you. I am going there to prepare a place for you. And if I go and prepare a place for you, I will come back and take you to be with me that you also may be where I am. You know the way to the place where I am going.'"

Mr. Li paused and looked at Afif. "Where is Jesus now, and what will he do in the future?"

"He is in heaven, and he will return again. Islam teaches this."

"If he is in heaven, then where is his kingdom? The place that he is preparing for his followers."

"It must be in heaven," Afif said thoughtfully.

"And he is going to return and take his followers to the place he is preparing."

"This is very interesting. I've never heard this."

"A moment ago, you compared Jesus' kingdom with Muhammad's. Muhammad was a great earthly ruler. He was a great leader. His people fought many battles. He was a success in the eyes of the world." Mr. Li smiled. "But Jesus wasn't interested in this kind of kingdom. He was going to prepare a place for his followers that would be out of this world. In another place. A kingdom that would have no end."

"This must be paradise."

"No, it is not paradise. He didn't promise his followers food and women. Those are earthly things. Jesus told us that in his kingdom, there is no taking and giving in marriage. This is to have children and to enjoy our earthly experience. His kingdom is very different. He promises us that he will change us."

"Where does it say that?" Afif asked.

"Here in Corinthians: 'Behold, I show you a mystery; We shall not all sleep, but we shall all be changed, in a moment, in the twinkling of an eye, at the last trump: for the trumpet shall sound, and the dead shall be raised incorruptible, and we shall be changed. For this corruptible must put on incorruption, and this mortal must put on immortality. So when this corruptible shall have put on incorruption, and this mortal shall have put on immortality, then shall be brought to pass the saying that is written, Death is swallowed up in victory. O death, where is thy sting? O grave, where is thy victory? The sting of death is sin; and the strength of sin is the law. But thanks be to God, who gives us the victory through our Lord Jesus Christ.' What is this saying?"

Afif looked lost, so Mr. Li continued, "sleep here refers to death. But when Jesus returns, the dead will be raised. Those who follow Jesus will have new bodies, so that they can enjoy the new kingdom.'"

"This is all very new to me. I didn't know that Christians believed this."

"Let me tell you a story, Afif," Mr. Li began. The other men gathered around:

"there once was a young man who wanted to visit a Sheik. The Sheik lived in a tent in the desert, so he started out walking. Whenever he found a Bedouin tent, he would ask the way, and they would point him." Afif nodded.

"Eventually, he met a man walking in the desert. 'Can you show me the way to the Sheik's house?' he asked.

"'Sure,' the man said. 'I know the Sheik.'

"'How do you know him?'

"'I am his slave,' the man answered.

"'Can you introduce me to him?' the young man asked.

"'Yes, I would be happy to do so," the man replied, so the two of them walked along in the desert. Eventually, they met another man walking in the desert.

"The young man spoke first: 'do you know where the Sheik's tent is?'

"'Yes. I do,' the second man replied.

"'Can you take me there and introduce me?'

"'I would be happy to do so,' the man replied.

"'How do you know the Sheik?" the young man asked.

"'I am his son.'"

Mr. Li looked at Afif. "Which man do you think the young man chose to accompany him and introduce him to the Sheik?"

"The son, of course," Afif answered quickly. Then he scowled as he realized the meaning of the story.

"The food is ready," Mrs. Smith called from the stairway and the men crowded down the stairs to the living room.

As everyone was enjoying the food, Mr. Smith placed a box on the table. "I have some copies of a movie," he stated. "It's a movie about Jesus. They are free, so please help yourself." Everyone took a copy and thanked him. The men and women mixed and visited for a short while, and then different ones started to excuse themselves and leave. Mona invited anyone who was interested to come on Wednesday evening for a discussion about the Bible. Several said they might come.

Several nights later, the Smiths and David were visiting with Zay'id and Mona. While Zay'id was out of the room answering a phone call, David turned to Mr. Smith.

"I've been thinking about the Bible study. It sure is great that more people are coming, but I think that the group is getting too large."

"We were thinking the same thing," Mrs. Smith said. "I find it really uncomfortable. It's hard to open up and share with so many people."

"Perhaps we should be thinking of splitting the group into two," Mr. Smith added. "We could choose a new leader and start another group. That way, it would be more manageable."

"Should we have one group that is more aimed at seekers?" David asked.

"I was thinking of a women's group and a men's group," Mrs. Smith commented.

"I'm not sure," Mr. Smith countered. "I wonder if that would be culturally better, or if it would rob the group of the family dynamic. Right now we have couples attending together, which I feel is a real strength."

"Perhaps we should ask Zay'id and Mona," David replied.

A few moments later, Mona brought in the tea and sweets. Zay'id finished his phone call and joined them.

"We were talking about the Bible study," Mr. Smith began.

"Yes, isn't it exciting," Zay'id smiled. "It's so much better now that we have more people."

Mr. Smith frowned. "Actually, we were thinking of splitting the group into two."

"Why would you do that?" Mona asked, shock showing on her face.

"That way, we could have more intimate studies," Mrs. Smith offered.

"But it is so much better, now that we have more people," Mona protested. "I'm really enjoying the group."

"Mona," Zay'id interrupted. "Mr. Smith is one of our leaders. If he feels it would be better to have two groups, then perhaps we should consider it." Mona looked distraught.

"Why do you think a larger group is better?" Mrs. Smith was puzzled.

"I love larger groups," Mona said. "I feel much more secure—especially if they are all my friends."

"That's strange," David entered the conversation. "I enjoy small groups. When there is a large group, I tend to withdraw and just watch things."

"I noticed that," Zay'id said. "All of the foreigners seem to withdraw a bit. But we Arabs love large groups."

"Perhaps we could do both," Mr. Smith offered. Everyone waited to see what he was suggesting. "We could have a larger meeting every few weeks."

"Another picnic?" Zay'id looked pleased. "I really enjoyed the last one. It was a great day." Mr. Smith tried to look calm. He just remembered feeling impatient throughout the whole day. "Yes," Zay'id continued. "I can understand this. Our homes are getting too small for the larger group. So perhaps it would be better to split into two. Then we can have more picnics where everyone is present."

"But how do we split the group?" Mona asked.

"We must choose a second leader," Mr. Smith commented.

"Why don't you lead both groups?"

"That might be possible, but I think it would be good to have a second leader. Perhaps he could help me lead both groups, and then if I cannot make it, he can lead."

"This is wise," Zay'id said. "A second leader would be good. How do we choose leaders?"

"I think we should pray about it and ask God to show us who it should be," Mr. Smith said. Everyone agreed.

24

The restaurant was busy when Mr. Smith arrived. He glanced up at the balcony. Jamal was seated at the corner table. It brought back a flood of memories. *"I wonder what he wants this time?"* Mr. Smith thought to himself. *"Lord, give me wisdom."*

"Welcome back." Jamal smiled and motioned him to a seat. "You remember this table?"

"Yes, I was just thinking about our first meeting here."

"Well, I'm not going to test you today." Jamal chuckled. "I've already ordered our food."

After their food arrived, Jamal finally broached the subject that was on his mind. "I would like to talk to you about Haytham, David's friend. I don't trust him."

"Really?" Mr. Smith looked alarmed. "Why do you say that?"

"Well, he is a young man, unemployed, but he always has some money. He is always dressed well, and he conducts himself very well. He never has problems, and he always studies for the Bible study. He is trying too hard."

"I don't understand."

"Yesterday, I saw him when I was driving my taxi," Jamal lowered his voice, "he was outside of the Ministry of Intelligence building trying to flag a taxi. When he saw me, he looked the other way, like he didn't see me."

"So, what is so suspicious about that?"

"I think he is a government agent, watching us and reporting on us."

"But we don't have anything to hide."

"No, but the government doesn't approve of Muslims following Jesus. They feel that it will cause social problems, tribal strife, and social unrest. If the Muslim fanatics find out, they will create huge problems."

Mr. Smith looked concerned. "How can we know for sure? And if he is a government agent, what do we do about it?"

"If he is an agent, then he has already reported us." Jamal looked serious.

"Perhaps we should talk with him and get a better feeling about his situation."

"But who will do it? I don't really know him that well."

"Neither do I," said Mr. Smith.

"That is just it. He is always there, but he isn't really close to anyone except David."

"Perhaps we should have them over to our home, and I can learn more about him."

"That would be good," Jamal started. "But I have another idea."

"Oh?"

"Why don't you get him more involved? If he is a government agent, then he is only pretending interest. Why don't you get him to lead in prayer? Ask him to participate more. Maybe share his testimony. Maybe even lead a study one night. We can then see if he is really interested."

"That is an interesting approach," Mr. Smith said thoughtfully. "I'll have David and Haytham over for supper first and get to know them better. Then we will see."

"I've been wanting to ask you a question," Mr. Smith changed the subject. "I was wondering if you might consider becoming a Bible study leader."

Jamal looked shocked. "I couldn't do it. I don't have any training."

"I could meet with you the day before and go over the study with you. Then I will teach the first group, and you can attend. Then you can teach the same lesson to the second group. I think you can do it."

"Why me?"

"I've been praying about it, and I feel that you have a real concern for the members of the group. You are sensitive to people's thinking. And you are the oldest, beside myself. We can try it for a couple of weeks, and if you don't want to continue, we can try someone else." Jamal nodded.

A few days later, the first group gathered for their Bible study. Jamal was leading the meeting, and Mr. Smith was leading the Bible study. Jamal got everyone's attention, welcomed them, and then turned to Haytham. "Could you lead us in prayer, brother?"

Haytham looked very embarrassed. "I—I really don't want to," he stuttered.

"That's fine." Jamal smiled and he asked someone else. Later in the study, he quizzed Haytham about Jesus' death and then asked Haytham to relate to the group what Jesus' death meant to him personally. Haytham asked to pass. No one seemed to notice, but Mr. Smith caught on right away.

After the Bible study, Mr. Smith had the opportunity to say a few things to Jamal while the others were getting tea and cookies from the table. "I met with them, and I think you are right. His faith is very weak and I don't think he is really all that interested. But he did ask me a lot of questions about other groups in the city, where they are, who leads them, and what organization we belonged to." Jamal nodded.

As the group was dispersing, Jamal slipped up beside Haytham. "Could I have a word with you for a few minutes?" Haytham looked surprised but followed him back into the living room where Mr. and Mrs. Smith were cleaning up. "Look," Jamal started, "we know that you are reporting to the Ministry of Information." Haytham looked shocked. "We don't mind that you are doing this. Please be truthful in your reports. We are not against the government, and we are law-abiding citizens. We love God, and we worship him. There is nothing political or anti-government about what we are going." Haytham nodded. "We just want you to know that we love you and want you to be part of our group."

Haytham looked down. "I'm sorry I have been so secretive. My job is to report on your activities and find out everything about you. When I started, it was just a job. But now I've become interested in what you believe." Haytham looked up. "I can show you the reports I wrote. I've said nothing negative about you."

Jamal smiled. "We don't want to see the reports. We've done nothing wrong, and we wouldn't want to be angry with you if you lied to us. Keep your reports. Just know that we love you and are concerned about you. If you need help or anything, we are here for you." Jamal stepped aside so that Haytham could leave.

Haytham nodded. He took his coat and made his way to the door. That was the last time that the group saw Haytham.

Jamal's taxi arrived first. The Smith's car arrived a bit later. Soon, everyone from the two Bible study groups had gathered under the trees. A small stream ran nearby, fed by a small waterfall. At the foot of the waterfall was a small pool. The children were soon playing in the water and the adults brought folding chairs, blankets to sit on, and boxes of food from the cars. A small fire was started and a coffee pot was put onto the coals.

Everyone was happy. This was a very special day. After an hour of preparations, Mr. Smith called everyone together near the pool. Opening his Bible, he read several passages of scripture and gave a small devotional about giving your all to Jesus and following him with your whole heart.

Then he called Jamal to give his testimony. Following this, Mr. Smith and Mr. Li entered the small pool where they baptized Jamal. Asma was next, then Zay'id and Mona. It was a very happy occasion. Hot tea was served afterwards, and everyone waited until the food was cooked over the fire. After they had eaten their meal, Mr. Smith called them together again.

"There is a second reason for us gathering today," he said. "We want to wish Mr. Li God's blessing as he leaves us and travels home." Everyone looked at Mr. Li while Mr. Smith continued to speak. "Mr. Li came to this country five years ago now. He has been a faithful minister of Jesus Christ. As I look around this circle, many of you are here because of Mr. Li. He was your first contact with Christianity. Over the years he has served faithfully, and all of us will miss him. I thought it would be good if some of you could share with us about your relationship with Mr. Li and how he affected your lives."

Mona was first. "It seems like long ago and barely real now," she stared with tears whelming up in her eyes. "I had heard a story that Mr. Li told in the hospital. Some girls were talking about it. I wondered at the story and wanted to hear more. There was only one Mr. Li, and so I waited for a chance to meet him." Her voice became very soft. "He didn't know it, but that night I was thinking of suicide." Zay'id put his hand on his wife's arm and smiled, supportively. "Mr. Li told the story of the prodigal son. I was that son. I had so much sin in my life. I was unworthy, and I desperately needed to be restored. That was the beginning of a whole new life. I met Anna and then Mrs. Smith, and then Zay'id. Everyone pointed me to Christ." She paused. "I'm so happy today. Back then, I never imaged that I would be baptized as a Christian. Today I can't imagine anything else. Back then, I was dead. Dead to spiritual things. Death to everything, even myself. I never imagined that I could find my way out the other side. But then I met Jesus and everything changed."

Asma sat beside Mona and handed her a tissue. Then she spoke. "I always thought that I was better than my sister. She made so many stupid choices in life. I thought I was making good choices, but my life wasn't much better. I was unhappy. My marriage was unhappy. I was shocked when Mona got married. I was jealous of her happy marriage. And I started looking for ways to make trouble for her. I caught her reading a Bible one day, but Mona only showed me love. I couldn't understand it; until I heard one of Mr. Li's stories from Jamal. Suddenly, I was so confused. Islam told me to try harder, be better, and pray more. Christians told me to surrender and let God change things. I'm so glad I surrendered to Jesus."

Jamal and Zay'id soon added their comments. Mr. Li started feeling embarrassed. Finally, someone asked him to speak.

"You are all being too kind," he began. "When I came to this country, I was very unsure how to share my faith with anyone. I made lots of mistakes. Then I met David and together we made more mistakes." David laughed and everyone smiled. "I haven't done anything special. I've only tried to live out my faith. That's all any of us should do. I'm just very normal. However, there is something special. It's all of you. Each of you are very dear to me. I've prayed for you all, as have others. You are all my family, and I'm going to miss you very much."

"But you are going to come back," Mona said.

"Yes, this is just a visit. I want to see my mother and father and relatives, and of course my church."

"And eat Chinese food again," someone commented and everyone laughed.

"Especially eat Chinese food. And I will be back. So please, Mrs. Smith, keep some cookies for me."

The End

Missionary Story Two

25

Gui Chen buried his head in his hands and closed his eyes. For the last two weeks he had kept a smile on his face even though his heart was heavy. Now that he was alone, tears welled up in his eyes as emotions swept through his body. His mind flashed back to the events of the past year.

The people in his church back home in China had been proud to send him to the mission field. His wife Mei and his son Huan had stood proudly by his side as the pastors prayed for him. Everyone had given willingly and sacrificially so that they had the money they needed to travel to Central Asia.

Their first months in the capital city had been stressful, but they had also been good times. They met with other missionaries, lived in a small apartment, and studied the language. During that time, they had all been praying that God would provide a way for them to get a more permanent visa. They had received letters from home which were much the same: everyone was praying that God would provide for them a means of employment that would provide a visa so they could stay and minister.

And then they met Mr. Ruslan. Actually, it seemed that Mr. Ruslan had met them. Gui's mind flashed back to their first meeting in a local market. Mr. Ruslan had seemed very interested in him and had wanted to meet his wife and son. He had been very warm and had invited them to his home. After two visits, Mr. Ruslan had offered Gui a job. It seemed like God was leading them forward.

Mr. Ruslan told them of a store he owned near an industrial area. His shopkeeper had quit and now he was looking for someone to manage the store for him. Mr. Ruslan had spoken about the store in glowing terms—it was the only store for several thousand people. It was well stocked and even had an apartment attached to it. Yes, it was a small apartment, but it was cozy, and it was a perfect setup for the right person. When Gui had expressed interest, Mr. Ruslan explained that the store manager needed to live in the apartment and sell goods. Half of the profits would belong to the manager and the other half would be sent back to Mr. Ruslan.

Mr. Ruslan explained that he had good connections with the government, and that it would be easy for him to get the needed visa and permits. He would be happy to arrange everything.

After a time of prayer with some of the other missionaries, Gui had accepted Mr. Ruslan's proposition and gave him their passports. That was the last time they saw their passports. Whenever Gui asked about them afterwards, Mr. Ruslan explained that they were at a government office, or some other location.

But all of that came later, after that fateful day when Alibek, Mr. Ruslan's skinny employee, had taken them to the store. The events of that day were clear in Gui's mind.

Their first impression was that the area was very run down. And the store matched the dilapidated condition of everything around them. They had stood in the doorway of the small shop and stared in disbelief and shock. Suddenly Gui knew he had been taken advantage of. His instinct was to try and block the doorway so that his wife, Mei, and his son Huan could not see inside, but it was too late. Huan twisted himself through the door and made a face.

"What is this? It's not much of a store."

"It's a wonderful store," replied the skinny man with the white skullcap. "Mr. Ruslan is doing you a fine favor by letting you run this business for him. This is an excellent business. There are no other stores on this side of the factory. Many people do their shopping here."

"But where will we live?" Mei asked, looking between her husband and the skinny man that she didn't trust.

"Oh, we have a fine apartment for you here at the back of the store," the man said, pushing aside a dirty curtain. With a crooked smile, he welcomed them to their new home. It was a very small room with a door leading to a very small cooking area. The toilet was reached by going into the alley outside.

As Gui stared bleakly around him, Mei suddenly realized the predicament her husband was in. She turned to speak to Alibek, but he had stepped outside and was unloading their suitcases onto the sidewalk. As soon as they stepped outside to speak to him, he smiled crookedly and jumped into the vehicle. "I'll be back in a couple of days to check on you," he shouted as the vehicle roared to life.

As her husband looked forlornly around him, Mei realized that now was the time to act. "Huan, help me with the cases. Let's get them inside and then we can clean our apartment before we unpack." Gui had done his best to help, but his heart was very sad. After cleaning the back rooms, Mei found some tinned fish and some rice. They ate in silence. Then Mei turned her attention to the store. Gui was grateful for his wife's energy. She seemed to know just what needed doing. As they cleaned each shelf, Huan wrote down what goods were there. As nightfall came they had inventoried everything in the small shop, and things were looking much cleaner.

"With a little paint," Mei sighed, "I think this could look much better."

Gui waited until Huan was out of earshot. "But we cannot stay here. This is not what we expected."

"It's what God has provided," Mei answered.

Gui was usually pleased when his wife thought of spiritual things, but now her answer grated against his feelings. "I think this is a mistake. I don't think that God provided this. I think Mr. Ruslan is cheating us."

Mei looked at him. "We won't know that until we've been here a while. We must make the best of it." Mei smiled. "Think of Huan; we don't want to burden him with this right now." Gui nodded, not so much because he agreed, but because whenever his wife smiled and looked deep into his eyes he could never say no. "Besides," his wife added, "we prayed that God would give us a place to live and work in the middle of a Muslim neighborhood, and here we are. We can be thankful for that."

Gui nodded. He could also be thankful for Mei and Huan. They were two wonderful gifts from God.

26

The first couple of days passed without anyone coming into the shop. Every morning Gui unlocked the door to the shop and greeted people whenever he saw them on the street, but no one stopped at the store. Gui wondered if it was because they were unused to the store being opened, or if it was because he and his wife were from a Chinese background. After all, he had not seen any Chinese storekeepers in the capital city. Then again, perhaps it was because of the high prices that were listed in the store. Gui didn't know the true price for everything, but he changed the prices on the goods to resemble what he knew from his time living in the capital city. It would be unfair to charge people more just because they were far from other stores.

On the third day, a boy came into the shop. He looked like he was about the same age as Huan. He was a bit shy but was looking for a box of soap powder. Huan had been sitting at the desk practicing his writing when the boy came in. Huan flashed a smile, something he had inherited from his mother, and quickly got the soap for him. When it came time to pay, the boy asked, "how much?" Huan did his best to practice his language, and the boy seemed surprised at the price. As he paid for the soap, he told Huan that his name was Askar. Huan smiled and told Askar his name. Gui stood at the back of the shop watching the two boys talk. He was proud at how well Huan seemed to be doing.

Later that evening, Askar returned with his mother. As his mother looked around the shop, Askar bought a bit of candy. "Where are you from?" he asked Huan.

"We came from the capital," Huan replied, "but originally we came from China."

"Where will you go to school?" Askar asked.

"I don't know. School hasn't started yet, has it?"

"No, next week we will start. Our school is just down the road. Can I show you?" Askar and Huan stepped outside. Gui watched them as they talked for a few minutes longer.

Later that evening, Gui and Mei discussed Huan's schooling. The following day, Mei took Huan with her and walked around the community. It was true, there were no other stores. Just a collection of apartment buildings, a school, and their one small store. On the street she met the same woman who told had visited the store, and she told her she was Askar's mother. Mei asked her about the school. Apparently the school was open in the mornings as the teachers were preparing for school. She advised Mei to go the next day and register her son.

The next day Alibek returned. His vehicle roared down the street and stopped in front of the small store. As he entered, the skinny man looked around in approval. "You've got it looking good," he said, pulling some papers from his pocket. "I've come to give you some advice." His eyes searched around the shop, then they returned to Gui. "Mr. Ruslan has a list of suppliers here. On one side he has listed the companies and their phone numbers; on the other side are the goods that they provide. When you need something, you simply call them, order, and they will deliver. You then sell the goods, and at the end of the month I will come by, examine your books, and collect the money. Mr. Ruslan takes half of what you earn, and you live off of the other half." Alibek's eyes bore into Gui's. "And he expects you to make a good living here," he said empathically, letting the meaning sink into Gui's mind.

"How can I call these businesses?" Gui asked. "The phone doesn't work."

"Mr. Ruslan will take care of that," Alibek said with a wave of his hand. "He has connections everywhere."

Two days later, a man arrived from the phone-company and hooked up the line. "It's been a while since someone was here," he commented before he left. Gui wondered about that. The goods in the store were all non-perishable items. There was no bread, no fruit, nothing that wasn't packaged. Perhaps the shop had been closed for a long time. However, that would soon change. He and Mei had decided to invest their last bit of money into some fresh produce for the store.

Several weeks later, Alibek was back to collect Mr. Ruslan's share of the earnings. He scowled as he counted the money. "This is not good enough," he scolded. "You won't be able to live on this, and Mr. Ruslan wants more return on his investment."

"How are our visas coming?" Gui asked. "Can we have our passports back soon?" Alibek shook his head, "they are still at the government offices." This was all the information he offered. "Next time we expect you to have earned more money!" he said sternly as he got back into his car.

Gui realized that he should have expected this kind of treatment from Mr. Ruslan. He suspected that this was a comment he would hear much more of in the future. His thoughts were suddenly interrupted by Huan and Askar entering the shop.

"Father," Huan said excitedly. "Askar is going to listen to a special teacher on Saturday. He's invited me to come along with him. May I go?"

"What sort of teacher is this?" Gui asked, speaking to his son in the local language.

"It's a Muslim teacher," Askar said excitedly. "He is coming from the capital to teach us about Islam. All the young boys are expected to be there."

"Can I go?" Huan asked, his eyes pleading.

"I'm sorry," Gui said. "I don't think it will be possible." He smiled at Askar. "But please come by anytime and visit. We enjoy having you around." Huan looked disappointed, but he went outside with Askar, talking about something that had happened at school that day.

That evening, after Huan was asleep, Gui told his wife about what had happened that day. "You gave the right answer," Mei said, "but we must handle this carefully. Huan is very attached to Askar. They have become good friends."

"Yes, but we cannot have Huan attending Islamic classes."

"You are right," Mei said, "but we must go carefully. Ee want to be more accepted in the community. The ladies are starting to buy things from the store, especially since we have some fresh goods every day."

27

"Father," Huan asked one evening, "Askar has been telling me about Islam. He says that it has expanded over the entire world, and that it is the greatest religion in the world today."

Gui paused what he was doing to think for a moment. He recognized his son's comment as an important one. Many thoughts suddenly flashed through his mind. Was his son being influenced towards Islam? As a father, should he not be teaching his son more about the things of God? How could he protect, or better yet, how could he equip his son to answer the challenges that Askar was giving? Gui put down the things he was carrying and sat on a box. "Askar is right. From the very beginning, Islam has spread very quickly. Today it has spread all around the world. From what I understand, it is now the second largest religion in the world. Most Muslims think it is the largest, but it isn't. But being large or small isn't the important thing. It is the truth that counts."

Huan nodded, listening carefully to his father.

"Islam is a religion," Gui continued. "It is a system of beliefs and practices that Muslims follow. They believe that if they follow everything that their religion teaches them, that someday, when they die, they will go to Paradise." Huan waited while his father collected his thoughts.

"Huan, when a Muslim prays, which way does he face?"

"Towards Mecca, father, why?"

"Why does he face Mecca?"

"I don't know." Huan thought for a moment. "Maybe it is the Black Stone?"

"Yes, Muslims face the Black Stone in Mecca when they pray." Gui paused. "When Christians pray, where do they face?"

Huan looked puzzled. "Face? I don't think we face anywhere in particular."

"You are right," His father said. "God is everywhere. We can pray in any position, and God will hear us." Gui smiled.

"What is it, father?"

"I once heard a story of a man who fell down a well. As he was falling, he called out to God to help him. The man was falling head-first, upside down. And God heard him and saved him."

"That's funny," Huan giggled. "Praying upside down."

"The position of your body doesn't matter very much, Huan," Gui continued, "But the position of your heart is important. God wants us to honor him and respect him. He looks at our heart, not just the position of our bodies."

"When the Muslims pray at the mosque," Huan commented, "they all have the exact same position. It's like watching an exercise class. They all move together."

"There is great strength and encouragement in doing things together with others. One feels protected and assured that they are right when everyone else is doing exactly the same thing." Gui paused and looked at his son. "But it takes real courage to stand up and be different. Do you remember the story of the three men in the book of Daniel from the Bible?"

"Yes," Huan's eyes got big. "Yes, Shadrach, Meshach, and Abednego, they refused to bow down, even when everyone else was bowing down."

"And what happened?"

"They were threatened and when they still refused, so they were thrown into a fire."

"Did God answer their prayers?"

"Yes, he sent Jesus to stand with them, and he saved them from the fire."

"Islam may be a great religion that everyone is following," Gui said as he turned back to his work. "But just because everyone is doing something doesn't mean it pleases God. We must always be careful to read our Bibles and follow what it teaches us."

"Askar reads the Qur'an, not the Bible," Huan commented. "He has to memorize the Qur'an every day. I heard him recite something the other day, but he didn't understand it. It was all in the Arabic language."

"Do you understand the Bible when we read it?"

"Of course, father. It is in our language."

"The Bible has been translated into many languages. Since it is God's word for all of mankind, Christians translate it and make it available in every language they can. That is why we have a copy of the New Testament in the local language."

Huan smiled. "Can I show it to Askar when he comes over today?"

"By all means," Gui said, silently thanking God for the help he had given him in answering his son's questions.

28

The door opened and a man stepped in. Gui looked up sharply. A gust of wind followed the man in. Perhaps that is what made his arrival memorable, or perhaps it was his size. At first, fear flashed through Gui's mind, but it was quickly calmed when he saw the large man's smile.

"How may I help you?" Gui said weakly.

When he heard Gui speak, the man smiled wider. "You speak well," he said, "for a foreigner." Gui smiled. The man's eyes met his. "I am Ivan," he said. "I'm originally from Russia. Where are you from?"

Gui blinked. This man was very straightforward. He wondered what he was up to. "I'm from China," he said after a long pause.

"Welcome here," Ivan said, looking around. "You have a fine shop here."

"Thank you."

"Are you a Muslim?"

"No, I am a Christian."

"Very good!" The big man's voice boomed in the small shop. "I too am a Christian."

Gui's eyes widened. "That's wonderful," he said with a smile. "I didn't know there were any other Christians here."

"There are a few of us living here. We don't have a church or anything. The church is downtown. Sometimes we go, but usually we don't." The Russian man looked around. "Do you sell vodka?"

Gui blinked. "Ah, no, I have no vodka."

"I understand," Ivan said with a twinkle in his eye. "The last shop keeper didn't keep it out in the open. Those Muslims would just get upset. It's best to keep it under the counter." He paused. "But you do have something to drink?"

"Pepsi?" Gui offered weakly. "I've also got tea bags, and loose tea."

"Tea?" Ivan laughed. "I heard you were Christians, and I thought that I would drop by for a drink. A real drink. Well, never mind. You can come and visit me. We can drink together. Who knows, maybe we will get drunk one night. We Christians try to stick together in this neighborhood."

Gui was suddenly very confused. "You said you were a Christian, didn't you?"

Ivan seemed offended. "Yes, I am a Christian. I was baptized in the Orthodox Church in town. The priest knows me. He's baptized every baby in our family. He prays for us, and for our departed relatives. I am a good supporter of the church. I even helped pay for the icon of Mother Mary. And I fast. Although sometimes I cheat a bit, but who doesn't?" Ivan looked down at Gui. "Do you know the priest?"

"No, I have never met him," Gui answered, not sure how to respond.

"Well, the next time he is in town giving Holy Communion, I will bring him over. He brings Holy Communion to all our homes once a month."

Ivan left after buying a few goods and Gui wondered what he had gotten himself into. This was not what he expected from other Christians.

29

The two boys climbed to the top of the hill. With the wind howling around their ears, Huan and Askar looked down on the apartment buildings below. Beyond them was the huge dirty factory with its gray smokestack bellowing smoke into the air. The smoke made it hard to see the city beyond that. As they were looking down, Askar began to tell Huan about his Islamic lessons on Saturday.

"Sheik Ackap knows everything," he boasted. "This week he told us about how Islam made everything better. Before Muhammad came, the people worshiped many gods, and they fought each other, and stole from each other. Women were treated badly, and everyone was ignorant. But Muhammad changed all of that. He taught the people about Allah."

Huan was quiet. He didn't know what to say to Askar, and he didn't want to offend his friend. He knew that his own family were Christians, and that they worshiped Jesus, but he didn't know how Muhammad fit into the picture.

"Muhammad was the last and greatest of the prophets," Askar boasted. "He conquered many people, had great riches, and was a great ruler. He was the greatest ruler this world has ever seen." Askar looked at Huan. "It's too bad you cannot come. Sheik Ackap tells wonderful stories. I'm really glad I can take Islamic lessons."

Down in the town below them Gui and Mei were discussing their situation. They had not seen Mr. Ruslan since taking over the management of the store for him. They knew little of what was happening other than the monthly visits by the skinny man, Alibek, who always demanded more money. Gui was beginning to cringe whenever he thought of his coming. Mei had her own reasons for not liking Alibek. While she didn't like his attitude, she also was becoming aware of the way that he looked at her when Gui's attention was elsewhere. She did her best to quell her fears and stay busy at her work.

"Maybe we should find work somewhere else," Gui said. "But first, I need to pay Mr. Ruslan back for the money he loaned us at the beginning. Then we could leave." He paused. "Except Mr. Ruslan has our passports." Mei's wide eyes met his and for a moment they stared at each other. Gui shook his head as if to clear it. "We must be wrong. Let's see if we can save the money that Mr. Ruslan paid us, and then we can move away."

30

As soon as school was out Askar and Huan gathered their things into their schoolbags. Strapping them onto their backs, the two boys headed for home. First, they would stop at Huan's house at the back of the store and then Askar would continue home. Askar had arranged with his mother that he could visit with Huan for a while after school. She agreed because she was happy to have Askar away from home for a bit longer in the afternoon and Huan's family seemed a good one.

This day, as they walked along, Askar began speaking about the lessons he was taking at the mosque.

"Did you know the prophet Muhammad had more than one wife?" Askar asked.

"No, I hadn't heard that," Huan answered truthfully.

"Muslim men are allowed four wives, but only if they can afford them. Muhammad, however, had many wives. That's how great he was."

"How many wives did he have?" Hunan asked.

"I don't know, maybe ten or twelve. Can you imagine that?"

"That's funny," Huan giggled.

"What is?"

"Imagine having ten or twelve mothers!" Huan laughed. "My mom is always asking me to do this or do that..." He paused. "Imagine ten mothers all asking you to do things."

Askar laughed. "Yes, that would be funny. But imagine having lots of brothers and sisters. They could all do things as well."

"Did Muhammad have lots of children?"

"I'm not sure; I don't think so."

"But if he had lots of wives, shouldn't he have had lots of kids?"

"Maybe."

"Christians only have one wife. I've never heard of a Christian having more than one wife."

The boys walked on thoughtfully. "Yeah, most Muslims only have one wife as well. Unless they are wealthy. Then they have more."

"I think some people in the Bible had more than one wife."

"Really?"

"Yes, Abraham had several wives, and lots and lots of kids and grandchildren. I think King David also had several wives."

"So why don't Christians have more than one wife?"

"I don't know. I will have to ask my father."

As the boys walked along, the call to prayer began to be sung out from a nearby mosque. Askar sang along with the call to prayer. Huan listened.

"What are they saying?" he asked when the call to prayer was done.

"They are saying that Allah is Great and Muhammad is the prophet of Allah."

"Can you understand the Arabic language?" Huan asked in amazement.

"No, not really. But Sheik Ackap told me what the call to prayer means." Askar paused. "The Sheik told us that Muhammad was more than a prophet. He was a great ruler and a very wealthy man."

"How did he get so wealthy? Wasn't he a poor orphan as a boy?"

"Yes, but he died a very wealthy man."

"Was he a great merchant?"

"No, his men attacked other people. They got rich from the loot they took."

"Were they thieves?"

"No, I don't think so. They were at war with others. So they fought back and took their stuff."

Huan was quiet.

"Muhammad had a great army. They defeated other armies much bigger than theirs." Askar paused. "What about Jesus? Did he have an army?"

Huan had to think hard. He couldn't remember anything about an army. He would have to ask his father when he got home. "I don't think so," he finally admitted. "But there were five thousand people that came to hear him speak. And he fed them all."

Askar seemed impressed. "That's a lot of people," he admitted. "But didn't he have a great army? Didn't he defeat any enemies?" There was a long pause while neither boy spoke. They just trudged along, carrying their school bags. Huan wasn't sure how to answer his friend. Compared to Muhammad, Jesus didn't amount to much. He seems to have been just a loving man with good teachings. And he died at the hands of his enemies. He didn't defeat them like Muhammad did.

That night Huan told his father some of the things that Askar was saying about Islam. "Muhammad seems like such a great ruler," he said sadly. "I love Jesus, but Askar doesn't think much of Jesus. He only talks of Muhammad."

"Perhaps it would be good if you spoke more about the Bible and Jesus."

"I guess so."

"Perhaps you could tell Askar about the miracles that Jesus did. Do you remember the feeding of the five thousand we read about the other day?"

"Let's pray that God will give you an opportunity to share something about Jesus." Together they bowed their heads.

31

Huan was determined to find an opportunity to talk to Askar about the Bible. Askar was always talking about Islam and Huan wanted a chance to present something about what Christians believe. Earlier in the morning, his father and mother had prayed with him and encouraged him to look for the opportunities that God would open for him.

Throughout the day, he and Askar concentrated on their studies. Huan had no opportunity to speak about Christ. Then, as they gathered their books into their bags at the end of the school day, Askar mentioned his Islamic studies again.

"Sheik Ackap is going to teach us more of the Qur'an today." He mentioned.

"Do you understand it when you recite it?" Huan asked.

"It is in Arabic, the holy language," Askar answered. "It is important to memorize it in its original language."

"My book, the Bible, is available in many languages."

"Really?" Askar looked interested.

"Yes," Huan said eagerly. "It is important that people all over the world understand it. That is why it is translated into different languages."

"But don't people change it and make it what they want it to say?"

"My father told me that groups of men always do the translation so they can check each other to make sure that they have done it correctly."

"Wow, that's interesting." Askar said. "Is it like the Qur'an?"

"I don't know," Huan said, "I've never read the Qur'an. It is always in Arabic."

"But Sheik Ackap tells us what is in it."

"But what if he is mistaken or just wants to confuse you? How could you check it yourself?"

"I don't know," Askar said thoughtfully. "Perhaps if I study lots, I can learn the Arabic language."

"I can read my Bible without a lot of study," Huan said proudly.

"Okay," Askar said defensively. "So what is in the Bible?"

"Well," Huan started slowly. "The Bible is in two parts: the old part and the new part. The old part is about everything from creation to the prophets."

"So you believe that God created the world?"

"Yes."

"And did he make two people, Adam and Eve?"

"Yes, and they sinned."

"What is that?"

"Did wrong."

'I never heard about that before."

"They were thrown out of the garden because they ate fruit that God said not to eat."

"Really? Just for eating some fruit?"

"Don't you have that part of the story in your book?"

"I don't think so. Adam and Eve lived and had children, and their children had children, and so forth, right down until today."

"But didn't God judge Adam for doing wrong?"

"I don't know. I never heard about God judging us now, but I do know that he will judge us when we die." Askar paused. "And he will send all of the infidels to hell."

"Who are infidels?"

"People who don't accept Muhammad as their prophet and the Qur'an as their book."

"Really? Am I an infidel?"

Askar suddenly looked embarrassed. "I don't know." He paused to think carefully. "I don't think you are. God sent different books to different people. The Ingil was sent to Christians. Do you have the Injil?"

"I think we call it the New Testament. The Gospels."

"Well," Askar said carefully, "Then I think you are not an infidel, because you have your own book. Do you believe in your book?"

"Of course. The New Testament tells us about Jesus."

"Yes, he was one of the prophets."

"My dad says that he was more than a prophet. He was the Son of God."

Askar looked shocked. "Don't say that. God couldn't have a son because he doesn't have a wife. God is one."

Huan looked puzzled.

"So who was God's wife, if he had a son?"

"I don't know," Huan said slowly. "I never heard of God having a wife. I'm not sure."

"Then you should believe in Muhammad," Askar said sternly.

"I will have to ask my father about this," Huan said meekly. "He will know the answer."

Huan waited until later that night to talk to his father. Every evening, they read from their Bible and prayed. After they finished praying, Huan decided to see what his father would answer.

"Father," he said nervously, "I have a question." His father smiled and waited.

"If Jesus is God's son, who was his mother, I mean God's wife?"

Gui was surprised, but then he realized that his son was asking because of the things that the Muslims were saying. Perhaps they had talked about this at school.

"Huan," he said gently. "You know who Jesus' mother was, don't you?"

"Yes. Mary was his mother."

"Do you think that God needed a wife so that Jesus could be born?"

"I don't know. I don't understand it."

"Neither do I, son," Gui paused. "The Bible tells us that the Spirit of God came upon Mary and that she conceived her child, but through it all she remained a virgin." Suddenly, he thought of something. "Huan," he started, "did Jesus exist before he was born in Bethlehem?"

"I don't know," Huan looked puzzled. "I think so."

"The Bible tells us that Jesus is God and that He always was. He was at creation. He was with the three Jews in the fiery furnace. The Bible tells us that he came in human form in Bethlehem, but that he always existed, and will always exist. God the Father did not need to take a wife in order for Jesus to be born. God created everything, and he could create the baby inside of Mary. However, God did it, he did not take a wife."

Huan looked relieved. "I guess I just didn't know how to answer Askar's questions."

"But you tried, and that's what is important. Let's pray that God will give you wisdom to answer him better next time."

"Father," Huan asked quietly, "why does Askar's God seem so different from the God that we worship?"

Gui thought for a moment. "Perhaps that is because Askar and probably all Muslims see God as the great sultan or ruler. He does whatever he pleases. He is a great ruler who can do good or bad. He does whatever he wants, and man can do nothing against him. The Bible, on the other hand, teaches us that God is more than a great ruler. He is a loving father. He is still working out his will, but he does so in a loving way. The Bible tells us that God loves everyone, and that he doesn't want anyone to perish. Askar is following Islam and the Qur'an, and so he sees God as a great powerful ruler. We follow the teachings of Jesus, who has revealed to us the Father heart of God."

Huan smiled. "Now I have something to share with Askar."

32

Askar and Huan were becoming close friends. After school each day, the two boys would walk home together. They enjoyed joking with each other and kicking rocks in the street. They would sometimes rush home to ask their parents if they could go to one another's house for a visit. Today, though, they walked slowly, because Askar would have to study before he went to the mosque for his religion class.

"I sure wish I didn't have to go today," Askar complained. "You don't have to go."

"I am not a Muslim."

"Yeah, that's too bad," Askar said. "Islam is the greatest religion in the world."

Huan thought carefully. "There are many Muslims," he admitted. "But there are also many Christians."

"There are more Muslims," Askar said confidently.

"I don't know." Huan frowned. "I think there are more Christians."

"I will ask my teacher," Askar said. "He will know." Askar paused. "But maybe numbers don't matter. Islam is the greatest religion because it brought knowledge to the world."

"What do you mean?"

"Islam brought philosophy, mathematics, physics, astronomy, medicine, music and geography to the world. My teacher said that others think that they invented these things, but they really came from Islam."

"Really? I've never heard this."

"That's because you are not a Muslim," Askar boasted. "Islam is the greatest religion because it brought knowledge and understanding of everything. My teacher says that the Qur'an is the greatest scientific textbook in the world. All the knowledge the world has about technology comes from the Qur'an."

Huan felt confused and disappointed. The Bible seemed like just a story book compared to the Qur'an. Sure, he had never read it, but if it really was a great scientific book, then somehow it seemed better.

"Islam introduced astronomy. Muslim scientists named the stars and knew how to navigate by them long before people in the west knew," Askar continued. "My teacher says that when the Portuguese first sailed around the world, they took a Muslim navigator along to guide them. Without the Muslims, they would never have made it."

Huan was quiet as they walked along the street.

"Science and technology are only small things," Askar boasted. "Islam is all about military conquest. From a little place in the desert, Muslims conquered most of the world—and very quickly, too. Allah fights for his people." Askar punched the air and then leapt up onto a small wall and pretended he was sword fighting. Huan laughed and ran along the sidewalk beside him.

"Allah who-a el Akbar!" Askar shouted the age-old Islamic war cry as Huan joined him in a mock fight against invisible enemies. At the end of the street Askar ran off shouting over his shoulder that he had to hurry home for his lessons. Huan trudged slowly down the street to the store, wondering why Islam seemed so great and glorious.

33

Erjan was concerned about the new friend that his son had made at school. Erjan's son Askar had brought a Chinese boy home with him after school several times. He seemed a very nice and polite boy, but Erjan wished to visit the Chinese boy's home and meet his parents. Some of it was concern for his son, and some of it was the fact that Erjan said that they were Christians, but they did not seem at all like the local Russian Christians. Erjan didn't want his son to become too close a friend with a dishonorable family and, what's more, he was suspicious of storekeepers because they often dealt with the black market or sold alcohol.

Erjan's wife explained to him that the Chinese family ran the local store where the women bought groceries. So, Erjan decided he would take Askar along with him and drop by the store.

Gui was serving a customer when Erjan and Askar arrived. He immediately recognized the man as Askar's father and hurried to finish helping the customer so he could meet the father and son.

With a wide smile, Gui turned to them: "you must be the father of Askar." They shook hands. "You have a fine son. He often comes here to play with Huan."

As if called, Huan stepped out from the behind the curtain that separated the store from the apartment. His eyes brightened when he saw Askar and his father.

"Come, sit down," Gui said, motioning them to two white plastic chairs behind the counter. "Mei," he called for his wife, "prepare some tea—we have visitors."

As they sat and waited for the tea, Erjan looked around the store. It was small and simple, but well kept. Better kept, he thought, than the last storekeeper, who sold liquor and pig meat.

"You speak very well," Erjan commented as Gui finished helping a customer who only wanted a single item.

Gui smiled again. "We've been in this country for two years now, and I work hard at it."

"Only two years?" Erjan was impressed. Gui continued to smile but didn't offer any more information. They had spent a full year just studying the language and being in the store didn't demand a very wide vocabulary.

"So what all do you sell?" Erjan continued, looking around the store. Gui pointed out all of the dry goods and canned goods, and the fresh produce, most of which had been sold by this time in the afternoon. Erjan was glad that he was seated behind the desk. He could see all of the shop, even behind the counter, and there were no liquor bottles anywhere to be seen. He was relieved. Gui and his wife seemed to be honorable people.

"I'm sorry I'm asking so many questions," he laughed to cover his embarrassment, "but it seems you do not sell any pig meat."

"No, the people here are all Muslims. So, I don't sell pork or alcohol. I don't want to offend anyone."

The conversation then moved to religion. Gui confirmed what Erjan had heard. They were Christians, and from China.

"There are many Muslims in China?" Erjan said. It was more of a comment than a question. "But aren't most Chinese atheists? After all China is also a communist country."

"China is very large and very complex," Gui commented as the two fathers sipped their tea. They watched out the open door as the two boys laughed together outside the shop. "China has many different kinds of people. There are atheists, there are Muslims, and many Buddhists, and there are also many Christians."

"It is similar to here, then," Erjan concluded.

"Yes, but we have many Christians. They are Chinese, not Russians." Gui paused. "The Russians here are all Orthodox, but in China we are just Christians who believe in the Bible."

"You do not believe in the Qur'an?"

"No, the Bible is our Holy Book."

"I've always heard that the Bible was changed. Corrupted."

Gui rose from his seat to help a new customer that had just entered the store. "We shall have to discuss this sometime," he smiled. "Perhaps there was a corrupted Bible that someone saw, I don't know, but the Bible I have is a careful translation from original documents."

After the customer left, Erjan finished his tea and called for his son. They rose and shook hands.

"Please come any time," Gui offered. "I am here every day and would love to have you come more often."

Erjan nodded. It had been a good visit. Gui was friendly and an interesting person. He would come again soon.

Gui was smiling as they left, but he was also thinking. They would have to get a couple more plastic chairs. Perhaps, just perhaps, a small group of men could sit around the store in the evenings. It was something to think and pray about.

The next day, Gui was surprised to look up and see Mr. Ruslan enter the store. He was alone, without Alibek, the skinny man who came every month to collect the money. Mr. Ruslan looked around the store with surprise and appreciation. "The place looks clean and organized," he commented. "You are doing a good job here."

Gui smiled, happy that Mr. Ruslan seemed in a good mood. Quietly, he prayed and wondered how he could ask about their passports and visas.

Mr. Ruslan moved around the store, looking at the various products. Then he asked to see the accounting book. After looking through it for a few minutes, he leaned back and smiled. Mei had served him some tea, so he sipped the hot liquid and looked at Gui.

"You've done well here, better than what I expected." He commented. "But you could do better."

Gui waited, wondering what was coming next. Perhaps this would be another lecture about making more money.

"I think you should consider expanding your products here."

"We have already done this," Gui smiled. "We now have fresh bread every morning, and fresh vegetables three days a week."

"Bah," Ruslan made a face and waved his hands. "Bread and vegetables are nothing. I'm talking about making some real money." He looked closely at Gui. "You need to sell cigarettes and vodka. That's where the money is." Ruslan looked up at Gui. There was greed in his eyes. "You are doing okay for yourselves here, but you could do much better, very much better."

"But Mr. Ruslan." Gui protested. "These people are Muslims. They do not drink alcohol."

Ruslan laughed. "That's what you think. There are lots of people who drink here. You are missing a great opportunity. Here is a list of suppliers. Just call them and place an order. They will deliver the next day." He paused. "That's why I offered you this job. No one will object to a Christian selling liquor."

Gui nodded bleakly. Not so much in agreement, but because he now understood why Mr. Ruslan was so eager to hire him. Gui paused and then tried to change the subject. "I was wondering about our work permits and passports."

"It is all taken care of," Mr. Ruslan brushed off his question. "Your passports are safe in my office. I have completed all of the paperwork."

"May I have them soon?" Gui asked.

"Sure, I will ask Alibek to bring them out for you the next time he comes."

Gui tried to shake off the suspicion that Alibek would forget to bring them. As he said goodbye to Mr. Ruslan, he thought that it would be good not to mention the passports to Mei. There was no use in worrying her, as it was now out of their control.

Later that afternoon, Askar and Huan arrived at the store from school. While Gui took care of customers, the boys sat outside and snacked on some nuts. Askar took the opportunity to try and impress his Chinese friend with the greatness of Islam.

"Islam is spreading all around the world," he said excitedly. "Before Islam came, we were just a group of warring tribes. But now we are united by Islam. Sheik Ackap told me that all of Central Asia converted to Islam in only a couple of years. It was Islam's greatest triumph. And it was done without bloodshed. Islam is truly a religion of peace that unites mankind together." He looked proudly at Huan. "Sheik Ackap tells me that true Muslim protect those within their borders. Non-Muslims are Dhimmi, or protected ones, so it is my duty to protect you. So you don't have to worry about the bullies at school. I will do my duty and protect you."

He opened one of his books. "Do you want to hear me read the Qur'an? I'm getting better at it." Without waiting for a reply, he started to read in Arabic, a language that neither he nor Huan understood.

34

Huan waited at the street corner. His friend Askar was late and school would start soon. He wondered if he should wait longer or go to school by himself. He decided to wait just one minute longer.

After a moment, Huan reached down and picked up his school bag. As he straightened, he saw Askar walking slowly up the street.

"Askar," he called, "hurry up! We are going to be late."

Askar looked up, and his steps quickened.

"Are you alright?" Huan asked. "You look sad."

"My aunt is sick." He paused. "She is my favorite aunt, and the doctors don't know if they can help her."

"I'm sorry," Huan said. "Has your family prayed for her?"

"What do you mean?"

"Well, when someone is sick in our family, my mother and father pray for them. Usually they get better."

"Really?" Askar looked puzzled. "How do they get better?"

"We pray to Jesus. He healed many people in the Bible. And he still heals people today."

Askar didn't respond.

"Did Muhammad heal anyone?" Huan asked.

"Sheik Ackap never said anything about Muhammad ever healing anyone."

Huan thought he saw an opportunity. "My family and I have been reading in the Gospels, and there are many stories there telling how Jesus healed people. I can read you some at lunchtime."

"You have a copy of the Gospels with you?" Askar looked shocked. "Is it in our language?"

"Yes." Huan laughed. "I can read it to you."

Later at lunchtime, the two boys sat under some trees where they could be alone. Huan took out his small New Testament and opened it. As they ate, he read some stories to Askar.

"Does Jesus still heal today?" Askar asked.

"Yes, all we have to do is ask him."

"How do you do that?"

"We just close our eyes and talk to him."

"Really?"

"Yeah."

"Can you do it, or just your father?"

"I can pray. I do it every night."

"Can you pray for my aunt?"

"Sure, do you want me to pray right now?"

Askar nodded, so Huan bowed his head and said a short prayer for Askar's aunt. He closed by asking everything he had prayed for in Jesus' name.

Askar seemed happy, but a bit bashful. He grabbed his lunch bag and the boys ran back to the school grounds, laughing and joking.

35

It started slowly at first. Askar's father began stopping by the store in the early evening, and he and Gui would sit outside and enjoy the fresh air. Gui would attend to customers, but in between customers the two men would sit and drink tea and discuss. A short while later, Nurbolat joined them. He was a close friend of Erjan and soon the three began to enjoy this time together. Sometimes they gathered only twice a week, sometimes almost every day. Erjan enjoyed talking with Gui. He found the Chinese man a careful listener, and his replies were usually well thought out and full of wisdom. Nurbolat enjoyed the tea, and a place to visit away from his wife, who never seemed happy whenever he was around the house. Some evenings they were joined by several other men from the nearby apartment buildings.

Gui always had a pot of tea on and sometimes he would open a package of biscuits. They would often argue over who would pay for the biscuits. Erjan was careful to always pay for at least one or two packages, while Nurbolat seldom paid, but he seldom ate any biscuits. The tea, however, he enjoyed immensely.

During the fall season, the boys would often sit nearby and memorize their lessons. Huan had a quick mind, but he struggled with language vocabulary. It didn't take Nurbolat long to discover that, despite his lack of education, he could help the young Chinese boy, and he looked forward to each evening he could spend outside the store helping the young boy while the two fathers discussed deeper matters.

One evening their discussion turned to holy books. Erjan was adamant that the writings of the early prophets had all been lost or corrupted. While he didn't know a lot about his religion, Islam, he had heard this many times.

"Look," he insisted. "How can you trust those early writings? They are so old that they obviously were corrupted. Our Qur'an on the other hand has been perfectly preserved. It has never been corrupted or changed."

"How can you be so sure of this?" Gui teased gently. "Do you have an original to compare it with?"

"Yes, there is an original in Samarkand. And another in Mecca. They are exactly the same as what I have."

"Two original copies?" Gui asked in surprise.

"No, they are not original. The original Qur'an was given in oral form, right from the lips of the prophet. Peace be upon him. Others heard him and wrote it down."

"So these are copies of those who actually heard it and wrote it down?"

"Yes, I swear by Allah, they are originals."

Nurbolat suddenly looked up. "I have seen pages of the Qur'an in Samarkand," he offered. "They were in a museum there." Both men looked at him in surprise.

"You have seen them?"

"Yes, I was invited by friends of a friend to go. They are all written in Arabic."

"See, there it is. The originals."

Nurbolat looked nervous. "Actually, I think I was told that they were written three or four hundred years after Muhammad."

Erjan looked annoyed. "Well, then there is the copy in Mecca."

Nurbolat looked embarrassed. "The sign in the museum said that the Qur'an in Samarkand was the oldest in the world."

"Look friends," Gui interrupted, "what difference does it make if the copy is old or original?"

"What do you mean?"

"If it is God's word, would he allow it to be changed? Wouldn't he protect it?"

"Exactly," Erjan saw his opportunity. "It doesn't matter how old they are, Allah protects his word. It cannot be changed."

There was a long pause while Gui poured them more tea. He prayed for wisdom as he made his next comment. "If Allah always protects his word, then wouldn't the writings of the early prophets also be protected?"

Erjan saw the trap, but it was too late. How could he answer?

"Allah always protects his word." Gui went on. "People are always discovering old manuscripts. And when they check them, the writings of the prophets are always well preserved."

"But those were writings for people of other places. People who lived long ago. The Qur'an is for us today. It replaces what came earlier." Erjan picked up a biscuit. "There is power in the Qur'an. If you would only read it, you would be convinced and convert to Islam."

"But I do not read Arabic," Gui said softly. "I hear that they do not translate the Qur'an into other languages."

"This is true. It was revealed in the Arabic language. It is the language of Allah."

"Surely Allah understands my language," Gui teased gently.

"Allah is all knowing. He knows every language, everywhere."

"Then why doesn't he reveal his word in my language?"

"I will have to ask the Sheik about this." It was the end of the conversation that evening. The sun was sinking below the horizon and it was starting to get cold. The men gathered up their chairs and teacups and prepared to move them inside.

"Soon it will be cold," Erjan commented. "Maybe we will have to sit inside soon."

While the men sat outside in the evenings, Mei was busy minding the store. She tried to support her husband while he talked to the men. They often talked about religious topics, and she would overhear some of the things that were said. She was happy to help her husband in the evening, because the mornings were her time to visit some of the ladies in the surrounding apartment buildings.

It started with Roza, Askar's mother, who had asked her if the store could stock some local fresh vegetables. When Mei asked her how they prepared the food, Roza invited her to her house to prepare a meal with her.

"Bring your pot along," Roza said with a smile. "We will prepare the food, and then you can take your pot home and cook it for your husband and son." It sounded like a good idea, so Mei went with her.

They enjoyed their time together, and soon it became common for the two women to compare their meal plans and arrange times when they could prepare common foods together. Sometimes Roza and Mei were joined by other ladies from Rosa's apartment building. Mei enjoyed the times together, although several of the women smoked, and sometimes they sat around and played cards. Mei would try to direct the conversation, but she wasn't always successful. Sometimes the women made crude jokes and laughed about their husbands' performance in bed. Mei wasn't sure how to respond, and she withdrew from the conversation at that point. Once she dismissed herself with an excuse and went home. It wasn't long before Roza caught on, and she would often change the topic before it got too crude.

"What's the matter?" one of the women joked. "Are you becoming too soft to talk about these things, or has your husband completely stopped trying?"

Roza nodded towards Mei, and the woman's eyes widened in understanding. She turned to Mei. "Why don't you discuss these things? We are women here. We are friends. We don't have secrets."

Mei prayed for wisdom. "I am a Christian, and my book tells me to think about good and pure things. I don't really wish to know or discuss your husband or my husband in this way."

"Really! But what else is there for us women? What else can we enjoy in life? We have children and serve our husbands. Visiting here is one of the few things in life I can enjoy. My kids are in school and my husband is at work."

"Then let's think of other topics to discuss," Mei countered.

"Yeah, like what? Doesn't your religion teach you how to please your husband?"

"Yes," Mei began slowly. "The Bible says a lot about relationships between husband and wife."

"Really?" the woman was interested. "Does it tell you how to do it?"

Mei blushed. "No, it talks about the relationship that a husband and wife have. If you would like, on our next visit together, I can tell you more. First, I want to read and prepare a little."

"That sounds very interesting," Roza said encouragingly. "I would be very interested in knowing what your book teaches."

And so it began. Twice a week, the women would meet in the morning to prepare food together, and twice a week Mei prepared something from the Bible to talk about.

36

It was early in the evening when the men gathered at the store, but with a cold wind blowing they opted to sit inside rather than on the sidewalk. It was crowded as they sat around the stove at the back of the store, but they enjoyed each other's company. As the store was becoming more accepted in the neighborhood it was also becoming busier and Gui was having a harder time looking after customers while also participating in the nightly discussions. He wished the discussions would take place in the morning, but this was not possible since the men all worked at the factory.

This evening Gui was busier than usual, and he could not hear the conversation because Erjan and Nurbolat were speaking in very low voices. After the evening rush was over, Gui joined the men for a quick cup of tea, hoping that no one would enter the store and disturb him for a couple of moments.

"So what have you been talking about this evening?" he asked. Both men looked embarrassed.

"Nothing."

Gui smiled and looked from one to the other. "No, you have been very busy discussing something. What is it?"

Erjan looked around. There were only three of them in the store. He lowered his voice, "a while back, a man came in here to buy some rice. Do you remember him?"

"Yes, the man with the dirty coat? He has been in here a few times in the past. I believe he has a son in school about Huan's age."

Erjan looked alarmed. "Yes, that's him." He paused.

"What is it?" Gui asked with a smile. "What is the problem?"

"This man and his family—they are not good people."

"He seemed nice to me. He has always paid and has never asked for credit."

"He may seem nice, but trust me," Erjan lowered his voice to a whisper, "they are not good. Not good at all. Have nothing to do with him."

"But his son is in the same class as Huan. Sometimes he stops here to talk to the boys."

"That is exactly it. You must not let your son talk to him. Stay away from that family. They are not good."

"I don't understand," Gui protested. He was thinking to himself that he had come as a missionary to these people. He did not want to stay away from certain people. The man in question had seemed very friendly and Gui had thought that their conversations might soon lead to an opening where he could share something about Jesus. "I don't understand," he repeated, "what makes some people worse than others?"

Erjan looked around. Then he rose and took Gui by the hand and led him outside of the store. The air was cold and a breeze chilled both men. Erjan looked around. "Do not repeat this to others. I am telling you his because you are my friend, and because your son and my son are friends. Listen carefully: they are a bad family," he whispered. "They do things together—to each other. Even the boys are involved." He paused. "Especially the boys. Keep Huan away from them. And watch out for Askar too. I've made him promise that he would have nothing to do with them."

Gui was shocked. If he understood the accusations correctly, then it would be best to keep Huan away from them. After they reentered the store, Gui's mind was still reeling. "Doesn't Islam teach against these things?" he asked the men.

They both shrugged. They then started discussing between them. Gui listened, but he only understood a few of the words. Another customer entered the store, so Gui was busy while the men finished their discussion.

When he returned, the two men tried to explain what they were discussing. The vocabulary was hard for Gui to follow. But eventually he understood that there were three kinds of sin in Islam. First, there were mortal sins called 'mufsid.' These were sins that were the most corrupting. Second there were sins that were 'haram,' or forbidden. Finally there were sins that were 'makruh,' or simply unclean. It took a lot of explaining for Gui to understand this and by the end of the explanation he was exhausted. The men hadn't told him what category the activities of the 'bad family' fell under. From their discussion he understood that the two men were not in agreement.

"Doesn't the Qur'an say anything about this?" he asked them. "If something is forbidden, isn't it written in the Qur'an?"

"Not always," Erjan answered carefully. "Many things are written in the hadiths, or the traditions of what the prophet Muhammad did." He then went on to explain that there were several books of hadiths that Muslims lived their lives by. These were as important to them as the Qur'an. "After all, the Qur'an gives us the revelations of Allah, but the Hadiths guide us in how we are to live our lives. We must emulate the prophet Muhammad. Peace be upon him. His life teaches us how to live our lives."

After the men left and Gui locked up the store he paused to think about what had been discussed that evening. The shock was wearing off and he wondered what his reaction should be if the man they had discussed came back to the store. No, not if, but when! And what would he say if his son came and wanted to play with Huan?

The next morning, Mei saw Huan off to school and then she quickly tidied up the apartment before getting her things together.

"Are you visiting the ladies again this morning?" Gui asked with a smile.

"Yes, you visit the men at night, and I visit the ladies this morning. I am preparing a Bible study for them."

"Really? That's much faster than what is happening with the men."

"Well, if I don't direct the conversation, then the conversation can turn to immoral topics."

"Really?" Gui was suddenly quiet. "This was not expected. I thought Roza and Erjan were good people."

"I think they are. It is mostly the other women. But Roza doesn't stop them. So we are doing a study on men and women in the Bible."

"Really?" Gui looked surprised. "What are you using as a guide?"

"Just the Bible," Rosa laughed when she saw her husband's face. "It's just things that I learned while we read together; things about husbands loving their wives, and wives submitting to their husbands."

37

It was a beautiful morning. In the distance Gui could hear roosters crowing. Closer at hand birds chirped in the trees. There were distant noises of the city awakening. Suddenly, the quiet was shattered by the sounds of someone knocking. Gui listened, confused, but the knocking continued. Gui realized that someone was knocking on the front door of the shop. Hurriedly, he rose and wrapped his coat around him. The fall air was cold and crisp. Putting on his slippers, he padded his way to the front door of the store, where the knocking continued.

"Yes?" he called out while unlocking the door. "What can I do for you?"

"I'm sorry to disturb you, but we need tea, coffee, and supplies. There has been a death in the family this night, and many people will come."

Gui recognized the woman as a regular customer.

"Oh, I'm sorry," he said gently. "Who was it who died?"

"My husband's brother; he was very well known."

Hurriedly, the two gathered up what the woman needed. "I'm sorry, I didn't bring any money."

"I will write it down," Gui said, pulling out a notebook where he wrote down all the debts of those who couldn't pay. The book was slowly filling with names and amounts.

An hour later, Gui related the events of the morning to his wife Mei and Huan, their son. "I think it must be Kamal." Mei said. If it is, he was very well known and respected in this area.

"Perhaps we should do something?" Mei suggested. "I could slip over to Roza and ask her." Gui nodded. He had no idea what should be done, nor what was expected of them.

After Huan left for school, Mei left to see Rosa. A few minutes later, Erjan arrived at the store. He was well dressed and looking somber. Over a cup of hot tea, the men discussed the events. Kamal was a respected leader of his family and well liked in the community. As Gui asked questions, Erjan recognized that Gui did not understand how funerals were conducted and was asking what he, the storekeeper, should do.

"Right now, the whole family will have gathered. The men will take his body into one room and will wash his body. It is important to be buried clean." Erjan spoke slowly, staring into space while his memory went back to the family funerals that he had attended.

"Then the women will come in and see the body. They will weep and cry. It is always hard on the widow." He paused and looked at his good friend, Gui. He longed to say more and finally added: "perhaps she is feeling badly because not everything was good in her relationship with her husband." He thought of his own mother. "Now it is too late to fix that. He has gone, and she is left to wonder if she pleased him in this life." Gui didn't really understand, but he waited for Erjan to continue. He could feel the emotion in Erjan's voice. "She will never know until she stands at the gates of Paradise." Erjan paused while he collected his emotions. His voice was choked with emotion, "then the men will take the body, wrap it and carry it down the street, past the store here, towards the graveyard. Many friends and family will walk with them."

"Should I go?"

"Of course; when we see them coming down the street, we will wait until they have passed and then join the group. I will write a note for you to put on the front of the shop. You should let shoppers know why you are closed."

Since Mei had not yet returned, Gui agreed. "First, let me change my clothes," he suggested, and slipped back inside to find something more formal to wear. When Gui joined Erjan in front of the store, they stood and waited for the funeral procession. As they waited, Erjan explained some things about Muslim funerals.

"In the Islamic religion," he explained, "there is an open coffin. It is a box covered with a blanket and more like a long shallow manger, with four handles. The body is wrapped in a long white cloth known as al-kafin. The person's head is also wrapped, but with a separate piece of cloth. Then we wrapped his hands across his chest and, finally, his feet." Erjan waited for a moment. "The women will spend time with the body first, so the widow can say goodbye. Then the men take the body to the graveyard."

Gui and Erjan looked up the street as a car slowly came around a corner. On the roof-rack was a long wooden box wrapped with a blanket. Beside and behind the car a group of men slowly walked. Gui and Erjan joined the back of the solemn group as they walked down the main street towards the edge of town. Eventually, they turned onto a dirt road that led to the graveyard.

At the top of the hill the procession stopped and the men gathered around while the family members took the coffin from the top of the car. They then carried the body the last 100 meters through the gate to the grave.

The sheik from the mosque was waiting at the grave and the people crowded around. The sheik waited until the crowd had gathered and then he started chanting some Qur'anic verses. Finally, he finished and spoke directly to the coffin as if he was speaking to a living person, as sheiks all down through history had done since the founding of Islam.

"Kamal," he said to him, "you are the son of a servant of God, and you are a servant of God. Now at this very minute two angels will come to you asking you a few questions. They will ask you: what is your religion? Who is your prophet? What is your book?" The Sheik paused. "Don't be afraid. With no reluctance, answer them: Islam is my religion, the prophet Muhammad is my prophet, and the Qur'an is my book." When Sheik Ackap was finished, the men laid the body on the ground and began to pile dirt and rocks over him. Eventually they would build a small cement block covering the body.

Afterwards, Gui and Erjan returned to the store. Mei was back and had the store open, so Gui sat out front with Erjan. After pouring a cup of hot black tea for his friend, Gui started to ask questions about the funeral. "Was it typical? Did the Sheik always ask those questions?"

Erjan nodded.

"So where is Kamal now?" Gui asked. "Would he be in heaven?"

"Heaven?" Erjan looked puzzled. "When a Muslim dies, he goes to Paradise. Only the prophets and great men are in heaven. And then they are usually in the lower parts of heaven." He paused and looked at Gui. "The teachers tell us that there are seven levels in heaven. Some of the prophets are in the lower levels."

"So who is in the top level?"

"God dwells there, but men do not dwell there. None of them are equal to God, so they cannot dwell there."

"Really?" Gui asked. "Are there not angels there?"

"Maybe. I don't know. A great tree separates heaven from Paradise. God is in heaven but not men, because they would pollute it."

"Really?" Gui asked. "Won't men be different in Paradise?"

"Different? What do you mean different?"

"Well, I mean better—changed into better people."

"I've never heard of this," Erjan said. "I don't think anything will change except man's status. Men will have many wives."

"Wives?" Gui looked surprised.

"Yes, Muhammad promised us many women."

"This is very different from Christianity," Gui commented. "Our book teaches us that the followers of Jesus will be changed. We will no longer be married, nor will we have sex in heaven. Those who go to heaven will be pure, and will be able to enjoy God's presence, and will bring pleasure to God."

"How strange," Erjan comment. "Your Paradise doesn't sound like a very attractive place." He paused. "What is the Christian hell like?"

Gui smiled. "Christians will be in heaven. No Christians will be in hell. The Bible describes it as a lake of fire, with agony. The real agony, though, will not be physical pain but rather the pain of knowing that you will have to spend eternity separated from God and the wonderful place he prepared for his followers."

Erjan looked thoughtful. "Don't people have time to work their way out of hell? Can they not do their prayers and eventually be accepted into Paradise?"

"I think there is a great difference between Paradise and heaven," Gui said softly. "Muslims are promised Paradise, a place much like this earth, with earthly pleasures. Christians are offered heaven and a relationship with God because we will be changed. Those in Hell cannot ever work their way into heaven. That is what our time on this earth is all about. The Bible tells us that now is the day of Salvation. Now is the time that we obtain salvation. The Bible also tells us that as soon as we are absent from this body we will be present with the Lord. There is no time between, and no waiting."

"Will God not judge if you are fit for heaven?"

"No, I will never be judged about heaven. God already knows if I am going to heaven. That is one question I will never face. The very moment that I surrendered my life to the Lord Jesus Christ, and accepted him as my savior who died in my place, my future in heaven was made secure. The Bible tells us that many things happened the very moment I accepted Jesus."

"Such as?"

"The Bible says that God wrote my name in the Book of Life. The Holy Spirit of God also began to dwell in my heart and he has started to make changes so that each day I become more like Christ. At the moment I accepted Jesus as my Lord and Savior, my sins were forgiven, and I am assured of my place in heaven."

"This is impossible," Erjan protested. "No one can know if God will accept him for Paradise or not!"

"I don't know about Paradise, but the Bible clearly teaches us that we can know that our sins are forgiven. The Holy Spirit is in my heart and active in my life, and the Bible tells me that this is my 'seal' or assurance that my name is already written in the Book of Life. When I die, I will stand before God as a forgiven sinner whose name is already in the book of Life. I will enter heaven."

"How can you be sure?"

"It is written in the Bible. I trust the Bible. I have submitted to it and its teachings."

"And God will not judge you?"

"Actually, God will judge me, but not to determine if I am fit for heaven or not. I am going to heaven. This is for sure. But I will stand before the Judgment Seat of Christ, and he will examine my life to see how I used it for serving God. If I served God, I will receive recognition and perhaps rewards. If I lived only for myself, I will receive nothing extra—only admission into heaven."

"Islam and Christianity are truly different," Erjan said and scowled. "People here are saying that they are much the same, but everything you tell me is different and new. Are you sure you are a normal Christian?"

Gui laughed. "I am very normal. There are some Christians who think that membership in a church organization will get them into heaven, but I don't think any of them have read the Bible, or they would understand how wrong they are."

"I must think about this more," Erjan said, rising from his seat. "It is late and I have learned many new things. Perhaps we can talk of this again?"

"Certainly, I would be delighted to continue this conversation another time," Gui smiled. His heart was rejoicing as he watched Erjan leave. Tonight he and Mei would have much to discuss and praise

God for. He looked forward to their regular family prayer time that evening.

38

It was the middle of the afternoon and Gui was exhausted. The store had been extremely busy all day long. It seemed that everyone in the neighborhood had chosen that day to visit his store. Mei was busy helping people find the goods they wanted while Gui worked behind the counter, taking people's money, and writing up a list of the things that they wanted him to order. The list contained many items, including dried fruit, dates, and other items he usually only carried in small quantities.

Later in the afternoon, Huan arrived from school and began helping in the store. The crowds thinned out by evening and there was time to talk a little. "I don't know what is happening," Gui said as he wiped the sweat from his forehead. "It seems everyone was here today to do their shopping."

Huan laughed. "Of course, tomorrow is the beginning of Ramadan."

"Yes," his father protested, "but that is a month of fasting, not feasting."

"Not the way Askar tells it." Huan's eyes got big. "He says that during the day they do not eat, but once the evening comes, they visit each other and eat big meals."

"Just on the feast," Gui asked, "or is it every day?"

"Askar told me that it is every day."

"If that is the case, then I will need to order in more food supplies tonight," his father answered. He took his list to the phone and began to check through his list of suppliers.

Huan helped his mother lock up the store and together they entered their small apartment. Huan gladly helped his mother prepare some food for supper. He was looking forward to learning about Ramadan. The way Askar described it, it sounded like a month-long holiday.

The next morning, as Huan was preparing his lunch, his mother stopped him. "Since this is Ramadan, will the youth be eating at the school?" she asked.

Huan stopped and thought. "I think you are right. I doubt any of them will eat today. Not until the evening." He looked at the food he had already prepared.

"You should eat extra for breakfast then," his mother advised. Huan nodded. It was going to be a long time until the evening meal, so he sat down and started eating his lunch, even though he had just finished his breakfast.

That day the store was as busy as the day before. Gui and Mei served customers without stopping the entire day. The extra supplies they had ordered the night before arrived and were all quickly sold. Gui made more phone calls to order more food.

That evening, just before dusk, the last shopper hurried from their store. Gui and his family stood at the door of their store and watched the last stragglers hurry down the deserted streets. A few moments later, they heard the call to prayer from a nearby mosque. Soon all of the mosques in the city joined together in a call to prayer that signaled that the daytime fasting was over and the nighttime feasting had begun.

The men did not gather that evening. In fact, the store was completely empty. As the evening wore on, it became obvious that no one was coming, not even the men who used to sit around and talk. Eventually Gui gave up and decided to lock the door. Just as he was closing the door, he looked out into the street. People were starting to move around and Gui spotted Erjan and his son Askar coming down the street. The two men greeted each other while the two boys moved to one side to talk.

As the two men visited, the store gradually began to get busier with young people and children. They were mostly buying sweet drinks, chips, and candy. When Gui commented on it, Erjan laughed. "If you stay open, your store will be busy for most of the night." He smiled. "People like to stay up late so they can eat, drink and smoke. Lots of businesses stay open all night. My wife has an appointment at the hairdresser at 2:00 this morning." He shrugged. "This is life. Ramadan is a special month. It is a blessed month."

Gui didn't know how to answer, so he continued to serve his customers. When there was a break, he sat back down to drink some more tea with Erjan. Erjan poured him a fresh cup and then smiled. "Why don't you and your family come to our home tomorrow evening to break the fast with us?" He put the teapot down. "Come before the mosque call, and then stay and eat. Rosa is preparing a special meal."

Gui was happy to accept, not just because his friend was inviting him to his house, but more because he wanted to learn about the month of Ramadan. It seemed to be a difficult time, with people fasting all day, but it was also a happy time, like a great holiday, as they stayed up late and ate special foods.

The following evening Gui closed the store and, together with his wife and son, they made their way down the street to Erjan and Rosa's house. Erjan welcomed them at the door and invited them into the sitting room. Their apartment seemed very large to Gui who had now gotten used to living in the two small rooms attached to the store. Together they sat in the sitting room, but no one offered them tea, or even water. They sat and simply waited. They could hear Erjan and Rosa at work in the kitchen as they prepared food. Eventually Askar came into the sitting room wearing his best clothes. He looked very smart as he moved around the room, shaking the hand of each of his guests.

After he was seated, Gui asked Askar about his studies at school. Askar responded positively and then switched the topic to his Islamic studies on Fridays. This last week the Sheik had taught his students to pray.

"Here, I will show you," Askar said. He stood, looked around, and then faced a corner of the room. "Mecca is in that direction," he announced. "This is called Takbir i-Tahrimah," he said as he held up his hands behind his ears.

"What does that mean?" Huan giggled.

Askar giggled back as he stood there. "I really don't know, but I had to memorize it." Askar bent over with his hands on his knees. "This is Ruku." Next he stood with his hand by his side, then he knelt down with his hand on his legs. "This is Salaam," he announced.

"I know what that means," Huan said eagerly. "That means peace."

"And this is Munajat," Askar said as he raised his hands before him, with his palms towards his face. "This is when we can ask our petitions of Allah at the end of the formal prayer." Then Askar got to his feet and sat on the sofa. "Next week Sheik Ackap is going to teach us the words to pray."

"Will they be in Arabic?" Huan answered.

"Yes, of course," Askar answered. "That is the language that God speaks. We must pray in his language."

Just as Huan was going to protest that God would know everything, Askar's father entered the room. "In a few moments, the Sheik will call from the mosque for prayer. After prayer time, we can eat."

They listened for a few moments and then they heard it: the sound of the chant rising and falling across the neighborhood. The chant was in Arabic, which none of them could understand. "God is great," the chant called out. "There is no God but Allah, and Muhammad is the prophet of God."

At the sound of the mosque call, Erjan unrolled a small prayer carpet and stood at one end, facing Mecca. Then he went through the motions of the Muslim prayer, speaking the memorized prayers under his breath. He bowed, stood, knelt, and moved at the correct time, as his father had taught him, and as his father before him had taught him. When the prayer time ended, Erjan rolled up the prayer carpet and turned to them. "Now let's eat."

The two families gathered in the next room. Erjan passed around a small dish of dates, urging each person to eat several dates. "These are good for breaking the fast," he said. After they had eaten the dates and drunk water, Rosa carried a large tray into the room. They all gathered around and ate a meal of rice, meat, and bread. Since Erjan and Rosa were breaking the fast they ate a large amount of food. When they were finished they all returned to the sitting room for coffee. Once again, the conversation centered around Askar's Islamic education.

"Sheik Ackap has been telling us about the pilgrimage to Mecca." Askar's eyes shone. "He wants all of us to make sure that we go to Mecca at least once in our lifetime." He paused. "Father, can we go to Mecca sometime?"

Erjan blushed and looked away. "Perhaps sometime, son," he said, "but we must pay for your education first—school first, religion second," he said softly under his breath.

39

It was late in the afternoon when the three men arrived. At first Gui didn't think much of it. He assumed that the three bearded men were just customers. They walked around the shop for a moment and then the eldest approached Gui. He offered his hand and Gui shook it. "You are not from here?" the man asked. The other two men stood close behind, regarding him carefully.

"No, I've come from China," Gui smiled, wondering what was happening.

"Welcome," the man smiled, but the two younger men behind him did not smile. "You speak our language well."

"Thank you; I am still learning."

"My friends and I are visiting this neighborhood. We are encouraging everyone to attend prayers at the mosque tonight."

Gui nodded, wondering what to say.

"This is the holy month of Ramadan and we would like all the Muslims to gather and hear good teaching. My friend here, Muhammad, has been educated at Al Azhar in Cairo, and he will be teaching tonight." He indicated one of the solemn young men behind him. Gui nodded and smiled. The young man did not smile back. "Are you a Muslim?" the older man asked.

"No, I am a Christian."

"Oh, have you heard about Islam? Would you like to learn more?"

Gui looked puzzled. "I am Christian," he answered again.

"Okay, but what do you think of our prophet Muhammad, peace be upon him?"

The older man asked with such confidence that Gui suspected a trap.

"I really don't know much about Muhammad," Gui answered. "But I know about our prophet, Jesus. I can tell you about him."

"But what about Muhammad?"

Gui smiled, wanting to avoid a trap. "Ask me about Jesus."

"Okay," the old man smiled back. "Can we sit and talk?"

"Sure, but I have to serve customers when they come in."

The young teacher muttered something to the older man. The old man looked up. "It is almost prayer time and we need to return to the mosque. Perhaps we could return this evening after we break the fast?"

"Of course," Gui smiled. "My wife and son will be here to help me with the store, so I will have more time."

As the three bearded men left, Gui began to pray.

That evening, Gui waited nervously for the three men to arrive. He prepared items for serving tea and arranged the chairs so that they had room to sit. He wondered if his friends Erjan and Nurbolat would also come that evening.

It wasn't long before Gui could see the three men coming up the street. With a prayer in his heart he called to Mei that they would soon be there.

"Peace be upon you," the three men said as they entered the store.

"And upon you," Gui smiled back.

The men sat and the youngest spoke first. "Before we begin," he announced solemnly, "we want to remind you that there is fire." He looked Gui straight in the eyes. "Fire is promised to all those who do not serve Allah." He pointed to the big stove with flames flickering inside. Gui nodded solemnly.

The eldest man smiled at Gui. "We are here to tell you about Muhammad. He is our prophet." Gui nodded.

"Long ago Allah revealed his message to his prophet. Muhammad then gave this message to the people. It is a message for everyone."

"The angel Gabriel spoke to Muhammad directly," the youngest man added eagerly. "The messages he gave has become the Qur'an today. It is God's word for everyone. It contains instruction on how we are to live."

"All around the world, people are following the message of Muhammad," the old man said warmly. "We are here to invite you to also become a follower of this light. Islam is light and we are followers of the light."

"Remember," the younger man added, "someday everyone will stand before Allah. He will judge everyone. Those who have not accepted the light and submitted to God will be judged. Everyone who is not a Muslim will be sent to the fire."

"But you can escape the fire." The old man smiled. "You too can become a follower. Everyone around here is Muslim, but not all are good followers. Much teaching needs to be done here to help them truly follow the ways of Allah." He indicated the young teacher who was sitting quietly listening to the others speak.

"Muhammad was a great man," the younger took his turn. "He led powerful armies. He had many wives. Allah blessed him so that he became very wealthy. Today Islam is the greatest religion in the world. People everywhere are submitting to Allah. Even in China there are many Muslims."

The old man leaned in front of Gui. "But the greatest thing about Muhammad is that Allah revealed his word, the Qur'an, through his prophet. Peace be upon him. The book came down directly from heaven to the prophet. He received the book from Allah and has made it available to everyone." Gui looked puzzled.

"What is it?" the old man asked gently. "Is there something you do not understand?"

Gui looked across the store at Mei who was helping a customer. Her eyes looked worried and Gui knew that his wife was praying for him. He spoke carefully, not wanting to offend these men. "You say that this man received a book from heaven?"

"Yes," they all nodded in agreement.

"The book came down to him personally?"

"Yes."

"So, were there witnesses?"

The three men looked puzzled. Gui added, "I mean, who saw the book come down? Or did this man just make it up?"

"No!" the men protested, "he received his messages directly from Allah."

"Through the angel Gabriel," the teacher added. Gui looked at him. Until now, this man had been silent.

"So there were no witnesses?" Gui asked gently.

"What do you mean?"

"No one saw the book come down? The man just claimed it came to him? Who witnessed this?"

"There were no witnesses."

"That is strange," Gui said quietly. "In the Gospels we have four witnesses who witnessed the truth. Each one wrote his account. But you have no witnesses. This man just came out of the desert saying that the angel has spoken to him."

The three men looked puzzled.

"Well, tell me about miracles," Gui spoke gently and softly. "The prophet Jesus did miracles to prove he had a message from God. The lame were healed. Blind people could see. Demons were cast out. There were many miracles to prove he was sent from God. What miracles did this man from the desert do?"

The three bearded men looked at one another. Then the young teacher spoke. "The message itself was a miracle. No one could speak like this. It was a message from God. The language was beautiful. It was perfect."

"So, other than giving what he claimed was a message from Allah, there were no miracles?"

The men glanced at one another.

"So, how do we know he was a prophet? I mean, someone comes out of the desert and claims he has a message from God—should we follow everyone with a message?"

The men were silent.

"There have been many people who have claimed to have messages from God. How can I know that this man had the true message and not someone else?"

"But it was the true message," the young man protested. "Millions of people are now following the light."

"But what proofs do you have?" Gui spoke quietly. "How can I test this to tell if it was the truth?"

The men looked puzzled.

"First, there were no miracles, but the other prophets did miracles—many miracles." Gui paused. "Well, what about his background? All the prophets were Jews: Moses, David, Solomon, Abraham. They were Jews. What about this man? Was he a Jew?"

The men shook their heads.

"Well, what about the previous prophets? We have their writings and books, and they spoke very differently than Muhammad. That is why there are different religions today. Christianity and Islam are not the same. If they were, this man from the desert would have had the same message as the prophets before him. But he didn't." Gui looked them in the eye. "How can I accept that this man was a prophet?"

"Look," the young teacher's eyes flashed angrily. "We came here to invite you to join us. To follow the light. You have no right to speak of our prophet this way."

"But I was only asking you. I don't know about this man who came out of the desert. I am a follower of Jesus. He was a Jew, and he did miracles, and he was sent from God. Doesn't your book also teach Jesus was a prophet?"

The old men nodded thoughtfully.

"But there is only one way to paradise." The young teacher argued. "When we face Allah, he will ask us who we followed. We are followers of the light given through Muhammad, peace be upon him." Suddenly, all three men were talking at once, arguing that Islam was the only correct way.

"You will never get to paradise," the youngest said loudly.

"Tell me about paradise," Gui asked gently. The three men all started talking at once again. It was a beautiful garden. There would be rivers of milk, honey, and wine. Beautiful women would serve the men. Only the true followers of Muhammad would get there.

"So, will you be different in Paradise?" Gui asked.

"Different? What do you mean, different?"

"Will you be the same person you are today, or will your character be changed?"

"I don't know what you mean by different." The older man was speaking now. "We will be just like we are now, perhaps with younger bodies, but we will be the same."

"So paradise will be filled with normal men?"

"Yes, of course, but all followers of Islam."

"So what makes paradise any different from what rich people today enjoy?"

The men looked puzzled.

"If people are the same, then maybe we will argue over things in paradise. Maybe we will be angry with one another." Gui paused as he saw Erjan enter the store. Erjan's eyes got very wide when he saw Gui sitting with the three bearded men. "In my book," Gui went on, "we are told that when the followers of Jesus die, we will be changed. In the twinkling of an eye, we will be changed. Our old nature, the evil part of us, will be stripped away, and we will be changed into good people. Are the followers of Islam changed?"

The young teacher looked puzzled. "I have never heard of this before."

Erjan now approached the four men with a worried look on his face. The three bearded men watched as he greeted Gui. "Who are your guests?" Erjan asked politely.

"These three men are visiting the area, encouraging Muslims to attend the mosque," Gui answered. "When they discovered I was not a Muslim, they wanted to tell me about Muhammad." Erjan pulled over a box of cans and sat on it. Gui offered him some tea, but he waved it away.

"We were just finishing," the young teacher said. "We want to return to the mosque to meet with some others."

"It was nice meeting you," the eldest man said, but he didn't sound very sincere. The three men rose to leave and Erjan and Gui stood as well. "Wait," Gui stopped them. "Before you leave, I would like to remind you of something. It is something you said when you arrived."

The three bearded men waited patiently. "Remember," Gui smiled at the youngest man. "Remember, there is fire. We must be absolutely sure of what we believe. It would be sad to end in the fire because we followed the wrong person or religion."

"Yes, yes," the teacher waved his hand. "We need to go now." Erjan and Gui watched the three men leave the store. As they disappeared from sight the youngest man glanced back, confusion and concern on his face.

"I've seen these men before," Erjan sighed as they sat back down. "They are Shiite Muslims missionaries."

"Shiite?" Gui said.

"Yes, there are several types of Muslims. We have Shiite and Sunni, just like you have Orthodox and Baptist."

Gui was surprised. Where had Erjan heard of Baptists?

"These men are not only encouraging Muslims to attend the mosque," Erjan said. "They are trying to convince every Muslim to become a Shiite."

"What is the difference?"

"Well, the Shiites believe that Islamic leadership should come from the family of Muhammad," Erjan said as he poured himself a cup of tea. "The Sunnis have elected leaders."

The men spent the rest of the evening discussing what the various types of Muslims believed. Gui hadn't realized that there were so many different kinds of Muslims.

40

The month of Ramadan was coming to an end. Gui was looking forward to a break from the hectic pace of life. People would come to buy groceries until late at night. He complained one night to Erjan that he was getting tired of the late nights. Erjan laughed and told him that once the feast came he could open his store late and close early. Everyone would be visiting others, so only the children and perhaps a few mothers would come to the store in the middle of the afternoon. Otherwise, everyone would enjoy a three-day holiday.

The morning of the first day of the Muslim feast, everyone was dressed in their very best. Groups of people moved along the street, greeting one another and entering each other's homes. By mid-morning Gui, Mei, and Huan were dressed and ready to visit as well. Their first stop was Erjan and Rosa's house. Askar met them at the door and invited them to sit in their reception room. When Erjan entered, they all stood. Erjan shook hands with each of them, starting with the person to his right. Afterwards, they all sat and Erjan poured them each a very small cup of bitter coffee.

After greeting one another with the traditional greeting "may God bless your feast," Erjan passed around a plate of brightly wrapped chocolates. They drank a glass of tea and then another cup of bitter coffee. After 20 minutes, the visit was over and Gui stood, thanking them for the visit. As the family began moving down the street, Huan asked his father whose home they would visit next. They visited the entire afternoon and arrived home in the early evening. They had eaten only sweets and drunk coffee and tea all day. Huan was giddy with laughter. Obviously, he was a bit young to drink so many cups of coffee and eat so many sweets. Gui opened the store in the evening for a couple of hours and was surprised at the number of people who visited. Most of them were children or teenagers. After a few customers, Gui began to understand that many of the adults gave small gifts of money to the children. Most of the money was quickly spent on sweet drinks and packaged snacks.

The next day, Gui saw Erjan on the street and asked him about visiting. "How many people do you usually visit during the three days of the feast?"

Erjan smiled. "I try and visit at least twenty homes each day. Askar is staying home to entertain anyone who might come to my house. It is important for us to visit people so that they understand that there is peace between us. Drinking coffee in each other's home is a very important ritual, as it assures us that there are no hard feelings between us."

Gui looked surprised. "Can I visit people that I think might have been offended with me?"

"Sure," Erjan answered with a puzzled look. "But who would be offended by you?"

"I'm not sure," Gui answered, "Sheik Ackap and I had a discussion and I'm not sure if he was happy with me."

Erjan looked at his Chinese friend carefully. "That is just the reason why we have the feast. If you want to make sure that your relationship is good, visit the Sheik. That will communicate to him that you are not upset with him." Gui nodded and Erjan continued. "I have not yet visited him. Would you like to come with me?"

"Certainly, that would be an honor."

"That is what friends are for. Are you free now? I believe that he is sitting at home today receiving visitors."

Gui and Erjan made their way down several streets until they came to Sheik Ackap's house. The sheik's son welcomed them at the door and invited them into the sitting room. A group of people were already in the room so when Erjan and Gui entered they rose. Gui followed Erjan as they went around the room shaking hands with each one. The Sheik smiled but looked carefully into Gui's eyes when they greeted. When Gui smiled the Sheik relaxed and smiled also. Gui greeted him and wished him a happy feast. The Sheik smiled and returned the greeting to Gui. After greeting everyone Erjan and Gui looked for a seat. Several people remained standing as the others sat.

"Please, sit here," one man offered. "We were just leaving." Erjan argued with him, but the man insisted and several of the people left after wishing a feast blessing on the Sheik.

The Sheik's son brought them bitter coffee. After they had drunk, the Sheik spoke to Gui. "It is good to have you in our home," he began. "Anytime you wish to visit, our home is open to you. I have not known many Christians, even though there are some in our town. You are the first to come and greet me on a feast day. I am pleased that you have honored us with your presence."

Gui smiled again. "It is you who are honoring me with such kind words."

"No, really, I appreciate you coming," the Sheik continued. "I have always been interested in Christianity."

Gui's eyebrows raised. "Really?"

"Yes, there are so many things that I do not understand," the Sheik continued with a smile. For instance, Christians say they worship a trinity. But I understand that the word trinity is not in the Bible. For Muslims, it is easy. God is one, and we worship only one God. We do not worship three Gods."

Gui continued to smile, even though his mind was racing. Outwardly, this seemed like a very pleasant conversation, but Gui sensed that the Sheik was trying to trap him, and perhaps demonstrate his own superior thinking. After all, there were a number of other people in the room. Even though they were talking with each other, Gui was sure they were listening. Erjan, at least, seemed to be listening very carefully. Gui prayed for wisdom.

"You are right in saying that the word trinity is not in the Bible," he began, choosing his words carefully. "But the Bible has always presented God as a triune being. When God created the world, the Bible always uses the term "we" instead of 'I.'"

The Sheik nodded. "The Qur'an does the same," he acknowledged. "But in our language, this demonstrates the superiority of God. It is a characteristic of Arabic and other Middle Eastern languages."

Gui recognized the wisdom in the Sheik's answer. He was carefully sidestepping the issue. "The Bible also uses the term Father, Son, and Holy Spirit. This can be seen in Matthew 28:19 where it says, 'go and make disciples of all nations, baptizing them in the name of the Father and of the Son and of the Holy Spirit.'"

"Ah, yes." The Sheik smiled. "I understand that this verse is not in the earliest versions of the Bible. I have heard that it was inserted later, when the church decided to worship three gods instead of just one."

Gui suddenly realized that this was not going to be easy. He reached into his pocket and brought out his Bible. "Can I show you something from the Bible?" he asked.

"Certainly," the Sheik answered. "But first have a glass of tea and something to eat." Gui waited until everyone had been served.

"The Bible does not use the word trinity because it assumes that everyone understood that God was three in one. For instance, we might ask the question 'who raised Jesus from the dead?' You might not believe in the resurrection of Jesus, but the Bible clearly says in 1 Peter 1:21 that God raised him up. Listen as I read: 'through him you believe in God, who raised him from the dead and glorified him, and so your faith and hope are in God.'

"You might think that this does not prove anything, but what do you think of this verse? Jesus is speaking." Gui turned to John 10: 17-18. "'The reason my Father loves me is that I lay down my life—only to take it up again. No one takes it from me, but I lay it down of my own accord. I have authority to lay it down and authority to take it up again. This command I received from my Father.'"

"Jesus makes it very clear that he had the power to lay down his own life and take it up again. The Jews weren't guilty of killing him; he gave himself to them, knowing they would kill him. But Jesus wasn't alone in raising himself from the dead. Galatians 1:1 tells us that the Father raised him: 'Paul, an apostle—sent not from men nor by man, but by Jesus Christ and God the Father, who raised him from the dead.'

"And, finally, listen to 1 Peter 3:18: 'For Christ died for sins once for all, the righteous for the unrighteous, to bring you to God. He was put to death in the body but made alive by the Spirit.'

"This is confirmed in Romans 8:11: 'and if the Spirit of him who raised Jesus from the dead is living in you, he who raised Christ from the dead will also give life to your mortal bodies through his Spirit, who lives in you.' You might wonder why I read these verses. The purpose is to show that the Bible simply assumes that God the Father, Jesus, and the Spirit are all one and the same. The Bible uses them interchangeably. It was clearly understood that when the Bible referred to 'the Father,' it was referring to the one and only God. It is also clear that the Bible refers to the Holy Spirit as being the spirit of God, and that they are one and the same, for God is a spirit. He doesn't have physical hands and feet. And the same is true when it refers to Jesus. We Christians believe that Jesus is God revealed to us in human flesh. God was far from us, but he drew near to us in the form of Jesus."

The Sheik looked very uncomfortable and several men muttered something about shirk. No one answered Gui, and quickly someone changed the topic of conversation. Gui wondered if he had done the right thing.

As the two men walked back to the store, Gui asked Erjan about the visit. "What did those men mean by the word shirk?"

Erjan looked embarrassed. "Shirk," he said after a moment, "is the greatest evil a man can do. It is equating something equal with God. By saying that Jesus was equal with God, you committed shirk. Did you really mean what you said?"

Gui looked puzzled. "How can equating God with God be bad? If I equated a tree or a rock with God, I could understand people being upset. But I truly believe that God revealed himself in the form of Jesus. It is not shirk. It is what the Bible teaches."

Erjan nodded. "You and I will have to talk more about this; perhaps tomorrow afternoon? I won't be visiting until the evening hours, so I could come by the store and talk."

Gui smiled. "I would like that," he said.

41

The day following their visit to the Sheik, Erjan and his friend Nurbolat came by the store to visit Gui. They sat outside in the afternoon shade, drinking tea and watching the near empty street. It was the third and last day of the feast. Most people were sleeping or getting ready to go on visits in the evening. It was a good chance for the men to get together and talk. It didn't take long for them to get around to the previous day's visit with the Sheik.

"I don't think Sheik Ackap was too happy with your answer," Erjan smiled. "He probably thought it would be easy to convert you to Islam."

"Why is that?" Gui asked.

"Well, he has been teaching us that most Christians would convert and become Muslim, but their leaders keep them from converting. But here you are in our town, with no Christian leaders around, and you are resisting his efforts."

Gui laughed. "It will take more than that to convert me."

"What will it take?" Nurbolat asked with a smile. "Perhaps we can find you a pretty second wife?"

"No," Gui looked serious. "I'm very happy with my wife. The Bible teaches us that we should only have one wife. Can I show you?"

When Nurbolat agreed, Gui went into the store to get his Bible. Erjan poured more tea. After a few moments, Gui returned and began flipping through pages.

"Why do you call it a Bible or holy book?" Nurbolat asked. "Is it the book given to Moses or to Jesus or to someone else?"

"It includes the books of Moses and also the prophets and the gospels in it," Gui answered.

"But they have all been lost!" Erjan interrupted.

"No, we have them."

"But they have been changed," Erjan insisted.

"Who says? How do you know?" Gui asked. There was silence, and then Erjan took the Bible and began looking through it.

"I don't know about this book," he began slowly. "Our Qur'an is God's Book. God speaks directly to us or to the prophet. But this book—it looks like a storybook." He paused and flipped through more pages. "This cannot be the book that God sent down for the Christians."

"Why do you say that?" Gui asked.

"Look," Nurbolat leaned forward. "There were 104 different books that came from God to mankind. Each of these books was delivered by a prophet. Each of these books contained a message for the people or nation that the prophet was sent to. Thus, the prophets brought books. And the books were God's direct message to that people."

Gui looked puzzled. Nurbolat cleared this throat and quoted something.

"What was that?" Gui asked.

"That was Sura 35 verse 24. It says, 'there is not a people but a Warner (or messenger) has gone among them.' Sura 10 verse 47 says, 'every nation has a messenger.'"

Erjan interrupted him, "this book of yours is a book of stories rather than God's direct message to people." He paused. "Even if it is true, we do not need to read the prophets because they had books sent from God to specific people. The Qur'an, on the other hand, was sent to everyone, and all they need to know is found in the Qur'an."

"But the Bible is for everyone," Gui responded.

"Listen," Nurbolat interjected. "Moses was the prophet for the Jews; Jesus was for the Christians. Right?"

Gui saw his chance. "No! Not at all! Jesus wasn't sent to the Christians or to the West. God sent Him to the Jews. Listen to Matthew 15:24." He flipped through the pages until he found it. "'A woman came to Jesus asking for help. She was not a Jew. Jesus said to her: I was sent only to the lost sheep of Israel.' In other words, God sent him to people who already had a religion given by God. Then, at the right time, He sent Jesus' apostles to all the peoples in the world." Gui flipped over some pages and read, "'then Jesus came to them and said, "all authority in heaven and on earth has been given to me. Therefore go and make disciples of all nations, baptizing them in the name of the Father and of the Son and of the Holy Spirit, and teaching them to obey everything I have commanded you. And surely I am with you always, to the very end of the age."'"

Gui looked up. "First, Jesus sent them to those who believed in God and then later to those who didn't believe in God. He declared that His message, the Good News, would be proclaimed everywhere before the end of the world. Matthew 24:14 says, 'this gospel of the kingdom will be preached in the whole world as a testimony to all nations, and then the end will come.' Today, this task is almost finished. No matter which nationality or ethnic group you are from, the gospel message is for you."

"This is very strange," Erjan responded. "I've always understood that The Qur'an replaced the gospels, just as the New Testament replaced the Old Testament. The latest revelation is the best one."

Gui shook his head. "They should all agree. God doesn't change."

"That's right. And since we have the Qur'an, we can tell that the older books have been changed. The Qur'an is correct. The older ones have probably been changed down through history. That is why God gave the Qur'an. It contained the truth to correct the mixture of truth and error that had crept into the Bible."

Gui was startled. He didn't know how to answer. Erjan then pulled a small booklet from his pocket.

"Sheik Ackap came to my house last night and gave me this book. It claims that the Bible itself says it has been changed and is untrustworthy."

"Really?" Gui laughed. "That would be strange."

"Then can you look up Jeremiah 8:8 and read it to us?"

"Sure," Gui said. He opened his Bible and quickly found the spot. He read aloud: "'How can you say, 'We are wise, for we have the law of the LORD,' when actually the lying pen of the scribes has handled it falsely?'"

"There, see!" Erjan exclaimed "The Bible says that the scribes that copied it handled it falsely. So it cannot be trusted."

Gui suddenly felt defeated. It seemed that Erjan was right. He had been proven wrong. His face must have betrayed his feelings because Erjan became excited.

"See, your book is not trustworthy," he exclaimed again. "You should convert and become a Muslim. God sent the Qur'an to replace the older books. The scribes had introduced wrong things into the old writings. So God sent another messenger."

Silently, Gui cried out to the Lord. Deep in his heart; he knew the gospel was true. He knew he had been saved. He knew that the Holy Spirit was in his life. He couldn't reject everything he knew just because of one verse in the Bible. Suddenly, an old memory flashed through his mind. It was an old man who had visited their church years before to teach the scriptures. He could see the man's face now as he repeated over and over, "always read the verses in context." Gui looked up. "I've never really understood this verse to mean what you say it means," he said. "Let's read the surrounding verses to see what they tell us: 'why then have these people turned away? Why does Jerusalem always turn away? They cling to deceit; they refuse to return. I have listened attentively, but they do not say what is right. No one repents of his wickedness, saying, "What have I done?" Each pursues his own course like a horse charging into battle.

"'Even the stork in the sky knows her appointed seasons, and the dove, the swift and the thrush observe the time of their migration. But my people do not know the requirements of the LORD. How can you say, 'We are wise, for we have the law of the LORD,' when actually the lying pen of the scribes has handled it falsely? The wise will be put to shame; they will be dismayed and trapped. Since they have rejected the word of the LORD, what kind of wisdom do they have? Therefore, I will give their wives to other men and their fields to new owners. From the least to the greatest, all are greedy for gain; prophets and priests alike, all practice deceit. They dress the wound of my people as though it were not serious. 'Peace, peace,' they say, when there is no peace. Are they ashamed of their loathsome conduct? No, they have no shame at all; they do not even know how to blush. So they will fall among the fallen; they will be brought down when they are punished, says the LORD.'"

Gui looked up. "The Lord is telling us that the people of Jerusalem have turned away from him. But they argue that they have the Laws of Moses, which they had! However, the lying pen of the scribes handles the law falsely. How can a pen handle a book if a pen doesn't have any hands? It is obvious that this is referring to the scribes handling the 'pure law' falsely, not altering the text.

"Verse nine clarifies this by saying, 'because they rejected the words of the Lord.' This is God's Law. In light of such rejection, what type of wisdom could they claim to have? We see that there is no mention that these scribes corrupted the Bible. If verse eight was claiming that the law was corrupted, then why is God calling it his word in verse nine?"

Gui turned the pages of his Bible for a moment. "Here is something that God says a short while later through the prophet Jeremiah. Listen to this: 'Say to them, 'This is what the LORD says: If you do not listen to me and follow my law, which I have set before you and if you do not listen to the words of my servants the prophets, whom I have sent to you again and again (though you have not listened) then I will make this house like Shiloh and this city an object of cursing among all the nations of the earth.' As you can clearly see, this passage mentions that you must follow the law, which God sent down, which was before Jeremiah! This eliminates any chance that this only refers to Jeremiah, since many prophets came before him. It also means that we must listen to the words of God's servant's the prophets, which God had sent over and over again. This was written after the verse about the lying scribes. God calls the people back to the law and the prophets. So obviously it wasn't changed."

Gui paused. "This morning our family was reading from Daniel, CHAPTER nine. Listen to what it says: 'in the first year of Darius son of Xerxes who was made ruler over the Babylonian kingdom, in the first year of his reign, I, Daniel, understood from the Scriptures, according to the word of the LORD given to Jeremiah the prophet, that the desolation of Jerusalem would last seventy years."

Gui looked up. "Daniel accepted that the writings in Jeremiah were true and that they were the scriptures. There was no time after this that the Jews or anyone ever questioned the authority of the scriptures, either the prophets or the Law of Moses. Even Jesus referred continually to the Law of Moses. There were many copies in circulation. It would have been impossible to change some without people complaining about it."

Erjan shook his head slowly. "It seems to say that the scribes corrupted the law, but you are right, they may have rejected it and written wrong things about the law. But that would only prove that God would need to send a new book."

Gui smiled. "Why are you so sure that your book hasn't been corrupted?"

Erjan said. "The Qur'an is trustworthy because God would not allow his word to be corrupted. He would always preserve his word."

Gui almost laughed. "So God has the power to preserve the Qur'an, but he did not have the power to preserve the Law of Moses or the Gospels?"

Nurbolat's eyes got big. "I understand what you are saying. If God could protect the Qur'an he could also protect the earlier books."

Erjan looked annoyed. "But the earlier books were for different people. The Law of Moses was for the Jews. The Gospels were for the Christians."

"I'm sorry to disagree," Gui said gently, "but Christians are followers of Christ Jesus. That's the meaning of the name. Before Jesus, there were no Christians. In fact, when Jesus was on earth, there were no Christians, only Jews and Gentiles. Acts 11:26 tells us that 'the disciples were called Christians first at Antioch.' This was several years after Jesus died. Before this, there were no Christians. Some were called people of the Way. Others called them followers of Jesus of Nazareth, or even Nazarenes. But Jesus came to the Jews."

As Gui was speaking, several customers greeted the men and entered the store. The evening was starting to get busy, so Erjan and Nurbolat rose and bid goodbye to Gui. "We will speak more of this again," Erjan said. "I hope we didn't upset you."

"Not at all," Gui smiled warmly. "It is always good to discuss things to determine what is truth and what is not truth. You are my good friend. I wouldn't want you to be misled, and I wouldn't want to believe a lie, either."

With that, the two men left.

42

The month of Ramadan was now over and life returned to normal. Most of the customers in the morning were women. Later in the afternoon, young people and men would come by the store. In the evening, people would gather on the street to chat and many stopped by for sweets, nuts and drinks. The chairs in front of the store had become a popular gathering place. There was a small eatery farther down the street, but other than this, there was no place for people to go.

When Erjan and Nurbolat came to the store, Gui placed two chairs near the counter so that they could have some privacy. When the evening mosque call started, Erjan turned to Gui and asked him if Christians prayed.

Gui was surprised and somewhat delighted. This was an opportunity to interact about something meaningful. "What do you mean by prayer?" he asked.

"Every day we Muslims pray in public," Erjan replied. "But as far as I can see, Sunday is the only time Christians pray. Even then, I've never seen a Christian pray."

"That is probably because we think very differently about prayer," Gui responded. "For us, prayer is talking with God. There are many times that I pray throughout the day. I do not need a prayer mat and I do not need to face any particular direction. God is everywhere, and he has promised to listen to our prayers." He paused as he took out his Bible from its place near the counter. "Can I read you something from the Bible?" The men nodded so Gui turned to Matthew 6:5-8 and read: "when you pray, do not be like the hypocrites, for they love to pray standing in the synagogues and on the street corners to be seen by men. I tell you the truth, they have received their reward in full. But when you pray, go into your room, close the door and pray to your Father, who is unseen. Then your Father, who sees what is done in secret, will reward you. And when you pray, do not keep on babbling like pagans, for they think they will be heard because of their many words. Do not be like them, for your Father knows what you need before you ask him."

Gui looked up. "Jesus teaches us to pray in a secret place where no one sees us. We pray often, whether you see it or not. We pray with the assurance that God is listening to us. We don't need to keep making repetitions. God loves us. Jesus came in order to give us a new relationship with God. Our relationship is no longer like that of a slave coming before his master, but like beloved children coming to their father. I don't want to give you the impression that this is some kind of exclusive privilege—it is available to you, too. You Muslims say you believe in Jesus. Well then, read his word and let him teach you."

Erjan was surprised, and his face showed it. "I never realized how religious you were. I've never seen you pray, so I thought that you didn't pray." Erjan paused. "How about fasting? Do you fast?"

Gui smiled, happy to be talking about Christian things rather than Muslims things. "Yes, I fast. Let me read some more from the words of Jesus." He read from a little farther down the page in his Bible from Matthew 6:16-18: "'when you fast, do not look somber as the hypocrites do, for they disfigure their faces to show men they are fasting. I tell you the truth, they have received their reward in full. But when you fast, put oil on your head and wash your face, so that it will not be obvious to men that you are fasting, but only to your Father, who is unseen; and your Father, who sees what is done in secret, will reward you.'"

Gui looked up. "Jesus teaches us to fast in secret so that those around us won't even know. God sees us, and that's enough. It's the same thing as with prayer. Our religious practices are different from yours because Jesus came to give us a new relationship with God."

"This is amazing!" Erjan replied. "We have just fasted for one month, and we tell everyone that we are fasting. But you fast, and no one knows it." He paused. "You are so different from what I expected a Christian to be." He shook his head in amazement. "I never understood how you pray and you fast."

Nurbolat leaned forward. "But what about alcohol? Why do Christians drink alcohol?"

Gui frowned, wondering how he could answer. Quietly, he cried out for God to help him. Then he opened his mouth and began to speak, letting God guide his words. "Alcohol causes a lot of problems and pain in this world. In some countries where it is banned, criminal gangs grow powerful by smuggling and trafficking it. Alcohol on its own does nothing. The problem is in people. When people drink alcohol, it lets people feel freer. And what comes out of those people? The bad things that are inside. The weakness of people is also demonstrated when they have trouble with the temptation to drink. We Christians believe that the Lord Jesus did not come to make laws that we impose on people. He called each follower to be responsible for his own actions.

"Listen to Matthew 18:7-9: 'woe to the world because of the things that cause people to sin! Such things must come, but woe to the man through whom they come! If your hand or your foot causes you to sin, cut it off and throw it away. It is better for you to enter life maimed or crippled than to have two hands or two feet and be thrown into eternal fire. And if your eye causes you to sin, gouge it out and throw it away. It is better for you to enter life with one eye than to have two eyes and be thrown into the fire of hell.'

"Whatever causes us to sin we must reject utterly. The people who go out and get drunk are not people following Christ. If alcohol makes us sin, then we should not drink it. That goes for other drugs as well."

Erjan and Nurbolat were both nodding in agreement, so Gui continued. "The Lord Jesus did not come to remind us of what it sinful, but to enable us to live differently. Look at what the prophet John the Baptist, whom the Muslims call Yahya says in Matthew 3:11: 'I baptize you with water for repentance. But after me will come one who is more powerful than I, whose sandals I am not fit to carry. He will baptize you with the Holy Spirit and with fire.'

"John called people to turn away from wrongdoing, but he announced that the Lord Jesus would give people the Holy Spirit—that is the power of God in their hearts to love new lives. He brings forgiveness for the past and power to live as we should."

"Okay," Nurbolat replied. "We both agree that alcohol is evil. But what about pork? Why do Christians eat pork? We Muslims do not eat pork because it is unclean!"

Once again, Gui silently cried out to God for help. Then he opened his mouth and spoke as God gave him thoughts. "People who want to please God have always been concerned with what is clean and what is unclean. In our hearts, we know that we need to be clean to approach almighty God. The Lord Jesus showed us a truth that surprised many people at the time and still does today. It is found in Matthew 15:10-11: 'Jesus called the crowd to him and said, "Listen and understand. What goes into a man's mouth does not make him 'unclean,' but what comes out of his mouth, that is what makes him 'unclean.'"' What do you think he meant?"

"Maybe man's spit?" Erjan replied.

"Most likely his vomit," Nurbolat countered.

Gui smiled. "That is what many thought he meant, but he explained it in verses 17-18: 'don't you see that whatever enters the mouth goes into the stomach and then out of the body? But the things that come out of the mouth come from the heart, and these make a man unclean.'

"God is talking about our words. The sinfulness of our hearts is much more unclean than any food or substance. As it says elsewhere in the scriptures, all food is clean if received by believers with thanksgiving and prayer. Our real need is to purify our hearts. God sent the Lord Jesus as the one through whom people become clean. This is demonstrated by the miracles that he did. For example, in Matthew 8:2-3 it says: 'a man with leprosy came and knelt before him and said, "Lord, if you are willing, you can make me clean." Jesus reached out his hand and touched the man. "I am willing," he said. "Be clean!" Immediately he was cured of his leprosy.' In Matthew 9:20-21 it says: 'just then a woman who had been subject to bleeding for twelve years came up behind him and touched the edge of his cloak. She said to herself, "If I only touch his cloak, I will be healed."'"

Gui looked up. "People who had conditions that made them unclean were made clean through faith in Christ. These miracles are signs for us, not just events that happened. God wants to make us clean. He wants to change our lives. This is the Gospel message. This is why Jesus came to this earth."

Gui was about to continue when several customers entered the store. As he was serving them, Erjan and Nurbolat rose. "It's getting late," Erjan said quietly. "We will talk of these things again." He squeezed Gui's shoulder. "I learned a lot today. Goodbye, friend."

43

Mei slowly climbed the stairs to Rosa's apartment. A few moments before, while walking on the street, she had felt fine, but as soon as she entered Rosa's apartment building tiredness swept over her. Was this a spiritual thing or simply something physical? A few moments later, Rosa welcomed Mei into her apartment. Several of the other ladies had already arrived, and the smell of hot tea and cigarette smoke filled the air.

Mei placed her bag on the floor and accepted a cup of steaming hot tea. It seemed that the ladies were already focused on a topic of conversation. After listening for a few moments, Mei realized that two topics were being discussed. One woman was talking about her son, who wanted a wife. He was looking to his mother to help him select which young women would be worthy of his consideration. So, this mother was asking about the eligible women in the village. Several names were suggested, and several comments were made. After that discussion had gone on for a while, another woman, Aigool, tearfully told the group of ladies that her husband was talking about taking a second wife. After the shock had settled, one of the women carefully asked Aigool if her husband had ever mentioned divorce. The tearful woman shook her head. "No, he's never mentioned divorce, but I'm so worried."

"Watch yourself all the time," one older lady warned. "Never be alone. Always be with another woman. Never give your husband a reason to question you. You must always have someone with you. We will help you."

"Yes," the women agreed. "We will help. You must always act in ways above any questioning. If someone is with you, then he cannot accuse you of anything."

"I remember a time when my friend was divorced," an older woman said emphatically. "Her husband gave her a cell phone. Then he later accused her of phoning men––but she didn't even know how the thing worked." Several women nodded and looked down.

"If there had been women with her during the day, then that couldn't have happened," one of the women added. "That's why we will try and protect you. If you go shopping, or if you are going to be in your apartment alone, please call us and let us know. We will be with you during this time."

"Do you have any idea where he is looking for a new wife?"

"No," Aigool answered tearfully.

"We will ask around," one of the women assured her. "It shouldn't be too hard to find out what he is thinking, unless he has connections outside of this area."

One lady leaned forward. "And when we find out who he is thinking, we will tell her what a terrible husband he is. We are your friends. We will work together to keep this woman away."

"I know what we should do." The older woman leaned forward to emphasize her words. "We should put a curse on the woman." There was a murmur of approval around the circle.

"But who will do it?"

"I could do it," the old woman offered. After a pause in the discussion she added, "or you could hire a professional." Immediately, there was a flurry of discussion as the women discussed who they should approach. Finally, they agreed. They would approach a woman they knew, but of course, she would charge money. After some discussion, they decided to each give some money so that they could pay the woman. They would want to accomplish two things: first, they needed to know who was this possible second wife. Then they would pay the woman to put a curse on her so that she would be influenced away from the marriage proposition.

As she listened, Mei's concern rose as she realized what was taking place. Silently she prayed, asking God to give her wisdom. Should she speak now? What should she say?

"Okay," one of the ladies said. "I know we don't have much money, but if we can pool our resources, maybe we will have enough. You may not have money now, but perhaps each of you can tell us how much you would be able to give. Then we know how much money we have to work with."

"I can give some." One of the women spoke up, and she mentioned a figure. It was a small amount of money, but as the ladies around the circle each told their proposed amount, the total slowly added up. Eventually, it became Mei's turn to speak. With a silent prayer in her heart, Mei spoke.

"I have been listening to you discuss this problem over the last while, and I agree with you. Something should be done. You are all right about this." Mei paused. "But as a follower of Jesus, I cannot agree with hiring someone to curse the potential new wife."

"Of course," one of the women smiled. "You can do it yourself. I knew of a Chinese woman who was very good. She could accurately tell fortunes, and could do many amazing things."

Mei was shocked. "No, it's not me. I cannot do those things. In fact, I refuse to partake in them. We as followers of Jesus have a different way."

"What do you do?" All the women were suddenly interested, many leaning forward intently to hear what solution Mei would offer.

"We pray." Mei said.

There was a pause. "That's it? Just prayer? Nothing more?"

"But how can you change things?"

"We believe that prayer changes things."

The women looked puzzled. The old lady laughed. "Prayer is required to please God. It is something good we do to balance the other things we do."

The women nodded. "So, how does prayer change things?"

"When Christians pray, we have God's promise that he hears us and answers our petitions. Jesus told his followers, 'Whatever you ask God the Father in my name will be granted you.' In another place he says, 'Seek and you shall find, ask and it will be given you, knock and the door will be opened to you.' When we pray, God answers." It sounded very simple and straightforward, and Mei tried to sound brave and confident, but inside she was terrified. What would happen if this failed? Everything she had said over the last months, indeed even these ladies' souls could be affected by this.

"Good," one of the women said. "You pray, and we will act. And we can see which one works."

"But how can we tell which one works?" another lady asked.

There was silence for a moment, and then one of the ladies spoke up. "We will try and find out who the woman is and curse her." She paused and looked at Mei. "You pray that the husband changes his mind."

Mei nodded and the ladies all smiled in agreement. Then Rosa served more tea, and they went on with their visiting.

When Mei returned home, she waited until there were no customers in the store to tell Gui what had transpired at the women's meeting that morning. Gui was immediately concerned. "I should ask around and see who the man is and which woman he is interested in. The men discuss these things sometimes, so I should be able to find out."

Mei waited until he was finished and then looked at Gui. "How will that help?" She paused. "I think we should just pray. We don't need to know. In fact, it is probably better if we don't know. We just pray. And when God answers, people will know it was God, not us."

Gui nodded. "I think you are right." He paused. "Perhaps we should fast as well." Mei smiled. This was exactly what she had been thinking. Soon they had agreed that Mei would still cook for Huan, and they would fast and pray for the next couple of day. They agreed they could drink water, but would abstain from eating.

"I think we should do more than fast and pray," Gui said with a sly smile. Mei looked surprised. "I will write a letter to our church in China and send it tomorrow. I think we need more people praying."

Mei looked puzzled. "A letter takes so long," she said. "Perhaps we should call them on the phone."

"Maybe we can pray about it." Gui paused, thinking about the money it would cost, and how many phone calls it might take before they got through to the right people. "How about we pray right now?"

Together they bowed their heads and asked God for wisdom to know how to contact the church at home. Mei asked God to help them be a witness to their neighbors, and to change the heart of this husband who wanted to take a second wife. While Mei was praying, the phone rang. She went on praying for a minute while the phone rang again and a third time. Finally, Gui got up to answer the phone.

Mei smiled when she heard Gui talking excitedly to one of their church elders back in China. Deep inside, she felt reassured. God had answered this small need. Surely he would change the mind of this husband.

44

Several days passed while Mei and Gui prayed and fasted. They did not know the name of Aigool's husband, but they prayed for him anyway. They prayed that God would make himself real to Aigool, and that God would change her husband's mind so that he would not take a second wife. They also prayed for all of the ladies that gathered in Rosa's apartment several mornings each week. Mei felt some fear when she thought of her next visit. What would the women say? What would her friend Rosa think? Mei was thankful that she could pray with her husband and that he was praying for her and supporting her in this. At the same time, they were both encouraged that their church in China knew of the situation and that there were others who were praying for them.

The next morning, Mei gathered her things into a bag. She had several copies of the Bible and some note paper in case the women gave her a chance to give a Bible study. Once again, Mei walked down the street and climbed the stairs to Rosa and Erjan's apartment. The boys were in school and the women were gathering for a social visit as well as to prepare food for their meal. The women had all agreed that today they would sort lentils, looking for stones or dirt. When Mei arrived, several women were already sitting around the small living room with bags of lentils near them. One lady had already poured the lentils onto a large tray and was swishing them around looking for any hidden stones or debris.

Mei joined the circle and was soon sorting her own lentils while listening to the women talk. Aigool had not yet arrived, so no one mentioned her situation, and everyone seemed to be happy with small talk while they sorted. As time went by, Mei began to wonder if Aigool was going to show up at all. Silently, she prayed for wisdom.

After an hour of visiting and sorting lentils, Rosa decided to serve some tea and biscuits. As the women stopped their work, Aigool and another woman arrived. Neither of them had lentils with them. Aigool's eyes looked red, as if she had been crying. As soon as they were seated, Aigool's friend broke the news. Aigool's husband was now threatening divorce. Some of the women gasped. An older lady sadly shook her head. Mei felt bitterly disappointed. God was not answering their prayers.

The old woman shook her finger at the rest of the women. "I told you this would happen. The only thing that will work is to have someone with power help us. I know a woman. Her name is Jadira. She can do it."

"Is her husband's name Borat?" one of them asked.

"Yes, that's his name."

"I have heard of her," one of the women said excitedly. "She is very good. I'm sure she will know what to do. We don't want to hurt anyone here, just fix the situation."

"That's right," another woman added. "It is not a curse we want, it is love we need. Can she cause Aigool's husband to fall in love with her again?"

"That's a wonderful idea," another woman added. "Perhaps she can do something for my husband, too." Several of the women laughed.

"I agree to getting Jadira," one woman said slowly, "but how will we pay? She can be expensive."

"Let's take up a collection," Rosa suggested. She rose and went to the kitchen, returning with a small deep bowl. "I will pass this around and each of you put in what you think you can give. Either give money or write an amount on a piece of paper. In the end, we will see how much we have." Rosa took a paper, ripped off a small slip and wrote a figure onto it and placed it into the bowl. One by one, the ladies either placed some money in the bowl or they dropped in a small folded piece of paper.

Mei was dreading what would happen when the bowel came to her. She could feel her face flush with embarrassment.

"I'm sorry," she said weakly. "I cannot agree with this. I do not believe in using any other power than that of God."

"All power is from God," the old woman snorted.

"I do not believe in this," Mei said simply as she passed the bowl to the next woman. "I will continue to pray for Aigool and her husband."

The next woman reached into her pocked and took out her small purse and dropped some money into the bowl. The coins clattered to the bottom, their sound seeming to demonstrate how much some of the other ladies disagreed with her.

Eventually the women finished their tea and they returned to sorting lentils. Aigool sat and watched them. The old lady paused in her sorting and looked up at Aigool. "Remember," she said wagging her finger, "always keep your money on your body...and your jewelry. Everything valuable you own should be with you twenty-four hours a day. You never know when your husband will decide to divorce you, and if you don't have your things with you, you will probably lose them."

Aigool looked devastated. Several women scowled.

Rosa looked up from her sorting. "I heard a joke the other day, do you want to hear it?"

"Yes," several women said, smiles on their faces, happy to be turning the subject away from Aigool's problems.

"One morning a man and his wife are having breakfast. The man says, 'Did you hear that the neighbor man is divorcing his wife?' 'No,' his wife answers, "why is he divorcing her?" "Because she has a big mouth," the man answers. The wife looks shocked and then answers––" Rosa paused and squeezed her lips together to make it as small as possible, "that's terrible."

The women all laughed and even Aigool smiled a bit. One of the women turned to Mei. "Do you have jokes about divorce in your country?"

"I'm sure we do," Mei said with a smile, "but I don't know any."

"But surely men divorce their wives?"

"Yes, it happens, but Gui would never divorce me."

"Don't be so sure," the old woman wagged her finger again. "You think you are pleasing him, but you never know…"

Mei smiled again, confidently. "We are followers of Jesus. We don't divorce."

The women all looked surprised. Then one of them brightened. "I know, it's the dowry! Gui probably had to pay such a big dowry, that he would never think of divorce and remarriage."

"That's the problem with dowries," one woman said bitterly, "if it is too low the man easily divorces you. If it is too high, he cannot afford to marry you." Several of the woman nodded in agreement.

Rosa turned to Mei. "So, how much was your dowry? Do you mind telling us?"

"Maybe he never paid a dowry," one woman suggested. "I've heard that in some countries men don't have to pay."

"That's terrible," one woman gasped. "The poor woman would have nothing of her own and no security."

Silently Mei prayed for wisdom. "Please Lord, give me your words to speak." Then Mei looked up and opened her mouth, saying the first thing that came to her mind. What she said even surprised herself. "Yes," Mei said, "Gui did pay a dowry for me. But the dowry he paid is not like the dowries here in this country." The women looked puzzled. "Gui and I are followers of Jesus. When Gui married me, he had to pay a very large dowry." Several women's eyes got big. "But it was not money." Mei smiled. "What do you think he had to pay?"

"Gold," several women said at once. "How much gold?"

"No, it was not gold. Something else."

The women looked puzzled. "Did he have to buy you a house?"

"Perhaps a car?" another woman added.

Mei's eyes twinkled. "No, it was not gold, or a car, or a house."

The women looked lost. "What did he pay?" they begged her.

Mei smiled at the women and then slowly said, "when Gui married me, he agreed to pay by giving me all his heart. He agreed that he would always love me, and that he would never love another." Mei paused. "This is the way it is with Christians. We give our hearts to one another and agree never to love another. The two of us become one. I have his promise and he has my promise, and we made these promises before witnesses. And that's the way it is between God and us. He desires that we give him our whole hearts." Mei looked past the women to Aigool. She could see the tears in Aigool's eyes. "Divorce causes so much pain. In the Bible, God says that he hates divorce. It is tearing apart what God has brought together. It is always painful. It hurts both the man and the woman, and it is devastating for the children." Several of the women were nodding.

One of the women looked up. "I've heard that in the Russian Orthodox church people have to wait seven years before the church will grant a divorce. Is this true?"

"I've heard the same thing," Mei said, "but I don't know it for sure."

"That's why some Orthodox men become Muslims," one lady stated.

"Why, so they can divorce their wives?" Mei looked shocked.

"Sure," the women chimed in. "It happens all the time. Lots of Christians become Muslims so they can divorce their wives."

"And marry Muslim girls," someone added.

"You are so lucky you don't have to worry about that," one of the women said to Mei. "I wish my marriage was like that."

Mei smiled. "It can be. If both you and your husband become followers of Jesus."

"Yeah, like that would ever happen," the woman retorted.

"I can pray for you and your marriage," Mei offered.

"Would you pray for my marriage?" another woman asked. Mei nodded, happy that God had helped her answer the womens' questions.

45

Rosa arrived at the store all out of breath. She had obviously been hurrying. When Mei had a moment to be alone, Rosa excitedly told her that Jadira was going to come to her house to meet with the group of women. When the old woman had approached her, she had wanted to meet with Aigool and all of the ladies to discuss what she could do for them. Rosa excitedly added that all of the ladies were going to meet the following morning at her apartment. "I know you don't approve of such things," Rosa added, "but I think you should be there to see the power of Islam first hand."

Mei nodded, but in her heart she wasn't really convinced. "I will try to come," she said to her friend Rosa, thankful when there were more customers in the store who wanted her attention and pulled her away from the conversation. She really didn't want to discuss it. She needed to pray about it and seek peace in her heart.

Later that night, Mei had a chance to speak to Gui about what was going to happen the following morning. Even though they had been praying and fasting for almost a week now, Mei did not feel peace or confidence in her heart. But as she prayed with Gui and heard him say that he thought she should go, she recognized that this might be an opportunity God was opening for them.

"Do you remember," she said to Gui with a slight smile, "when we first arrived here, we asked God for the opportunity to visit in the homes of people around here? And now I don't want to go. God has opened the door, but I really don't feel comfortable with what is happening."

Gui nodded. "But God doesn't always answer the way we expect. Remember the last visit? God gave you words to say. I will close the store and pray for you while you are there tomorrow. I will be praying that God gives you the words to say again."

Mei was so thankful to have a husband like Gui, who loved her and stood behind her. How different her marriage was compared to the lives of the Muslim women around her.

Later in the morning Mei gathered her things, making sure she had her copy of the Bible in Chinese as well as one in the local language. Hopefully she would have a chance to share something. Then she started down the street towards Rosa's house.

There was an air of expectancy and an excited atmosphere as the women gathered. They were all looking forward to Jadira's visit. Mei was uncertain what to expect. It sounded like Jadira was a strong woman who could do anything. She wondered what she looked like––probably some large tough-looking woman.

As the women sat and visited, they discussed various aspects of Islamic life. Over and over, they mentioned something about an "eye." When Mei asked, the women were surprised that she knew nothing about this.

"The evil eye comes into effect when someone is jealous of another person," they told her. "As a result, the person affected will experience some sort of harm."

"Anyone can bring the evil eye, even an unbeliever," one woman said. "If you are jealous, the evil eye will attack the thing you are jealous of."

The old woman spoke up. "The Prophet (peace be upon him) told us that the influence of the evil eye is a fact. If we say 'Masha Allah' (as God wills) when we see something appealing, it protects others from the evil eye."

"I like to recite some verses from the Qur'an," another woman said. "That also helps protect us from the evil eye."

"You can also burn incense to keep away the evil eye," another offered.

"The best way is to hang the evil eye symbol in your home," another woman commented.

"Bah," the old woman scoffed. "The best way is to burn garlic peels."

"You must also be careful not to spend too much money and show off your wealth or the things that you buy," Rosa offered. "That will also bring on the evil eye."

"When my son bought a new car," the old woman said, "I placed black seeds in the car. Those seeds were blessed by the Sheik with verses from the Qur'an. They worked too, until he had his car cleaned and the seeds were removed. His car crashed the very next day."

"Yes, you must never say anything good about anything," another woman offered. "One of my friends commented on my new eyeglasses and told me how nice they were. After a while, I accidently sat on them and broke them."

"Yes, the very same thing happened to me. I was breastfeeding my baby, and everything was fine until the nurse commented on how happy she was that I was breastfeeding. A few days later my breasts became infected."

"I remember once when we were all at my friend's house and someone commented on how beautiful the house and carpets were. Within an hour, charcoal from a hubble-bubble pipe fell onto the carpet. The resulting burn looked like an eye," the old woman said. "This was when we decided not to have contact with her again. She was too quick to say nice things and didn't think about others."

"I think the best way is to get someone like Jadira to make a charm to protect you. She specializes in praying over a child's shoe. It is then tied under the car so that the car never hits a child. And it works."

"Yes, the taxis all have a Qur'an in them to protect them from accidents."

"In our home, we painted the outside walls green, and put green all around the windows. That is supposed to help protect against the evil eye."

Mei was surprised as she sat and listened to these ladies talk about superstitions. She had thought that these were modern sophisticated ladies, but they all sounded like superstitious village women. She thought about asking more questions, but there was a knock at the door. Rosa answered the door and warmly welcomed Jadira into the room.

Mei was surprised. Jadira was a young, slender woman about Mei's age. She had a bright smile and beautiful eyes. All of the women were gushing about how happy they were to see her. Jadira made her way around the room, shaking hands and kissing the cheeks of each of the women. When she came to Mei she smiled and shook Mei's hand. "You are Chinese," she stated. "Are you a Muslim?"

"No, I'm a follower of Jesus."

"I've heard of you. You are the one who believes that your prayers are more powerful than mine." She paused, her eyes growing hard. "And yet I am the one invited here..." She paused again, nodded, and then moved on to the next lady. Mei felt defeated. It was true, all their prayers had done nothing. Mei found herself looking at the floor, almost unaware of the others in the room. Jadira finished greeting the women and they all sat down. Aigool began to tell her story. When she broke down in tears, one of the other women would continue for a while. The women now believed they knew who the other woman was. She lived in another area of the city near Aigool's husband's place of work. Eventually, they finished their story and waited for Jadira.

"I will write out a prayer," Jadira said slowly, speaking to Aigool. "You must attach this to your husband in some way. Perhaps slip it into his pocket. Sewing it into his clothing would be best. It will help change his heart." Jadira looked around the room. "I will write out another prayer, and one of you must find this woman and get the prayer into her home or on her person. Then she or her home will come to some harm." The ladies looked satisfied, so Jadira asked for a paper. Then she closed her eyes and began to chant the Qur'an under her breath, holding the pen above the paper. The room was silent except for the sound of Jadira's voice as it rose and fell to the rhythmic chant.

Everything inside of Mei was in turmoil. She wanted to say something or do something to stop this process. Her whole body felt like it was shaking. "Stop!" she blurted out. "I would rather you don't do this." The chanting stopped and Jadira turned her head towards Mei, anger filling her eyes. Mei continued, "do not hurt the woman. She is a sister like all of you are."

"You dare to interrupt me?" Jadira spat out the words in anger. "You do not believe I have power?" Her eyes flashed. "I can tell you what is said or done in another room. I know things. I can do things. Watch this." She pointed to a plate of biscuits and then slowly raised her hand. The plate began to rise off of the table with no one touching it. The ladies all gasped in amazement. Several clapped their hands together in glee. Jadira smiled triumphantly. "Can you do greater than that?"

Silently Mei cried out to God. "Please help me, I don't know what to say or do. I am going to open my mouth to speak. Please fill it with your words."

Mei opened her mouth and spoke: "dear Jesus," she prayed out loud, "please remove this power from this woman so she can never again do these things. I ask in Jesus' name, Amen."

The plate crashed to the floor, biscuits flying everywhere. Jadira swore and rose, gathering her things. In a moment she turned and rushed out of the door. The women cried out in disappointment and then turned onto Mei in anger. "You have chased her away." "Now we will never help Aigool" "Why are you against us?"

Tears rolled down Mei's face. She didn't know how to answer. One by one the ladies rose and left. Aigool looked long and hard into Mei's eyes before she left. Soon only Mei and Rosa were left in the apartment. Rosa was cleaning up the plate of cookies. Mei rose and silently helped her. Eventually Mei managed to speak. "I'm sorry, Rosa, I didn't mean for that to happen. I just couldn't approve."

Rosa turned to Mei. There was no resentment in her eyes. "My husband would have agreed with you. He says there is no place in Islam for this kind of thing. Perhaps you did the right thing."

Mei nodded. She gathered her things and turned to go. "Thank you for being my friend," she said to Rosa as she slipped out the door.

46

Mei was so discouraged. Three weeks had passed since the last ladies' meeting at Rosa's. Jadira, the Muslim lady who wrote charms, had rushed out of the meeting, and one by one the angry ladies had followed her. Even Rosa, who was always her friend, now seemed distant. They seldom saw one another, although their two sons still spent time together. Erjan still came by the store to be with the men in the evenings, but the ladies' ministry seemed to have ended.

After two weeks of prayer and fasting, and then the disastrous ladies' meeting, Mei had returned to eating. Daily life continued, but for Mei, something seemed to have died inside her. She was no longer full of zeal and enthusiasm. Now doubts started to creep into her heart. She had prayed and fasted and had trusted God to put the right words into her mouth. Her husband and the church at home had prayed and fasted. But none of it seemed to help. Everything that Mei had tried to do, the contacts she had tried to nurture, the ladies' meeting that she had started¬¬---all of this had ended in disaster. Secretly, Mei began to think of how much better it would be to return to China and be close to her family and friends.

Mei found herself going through the motions of supporting her husband and son, taking care of the household and helping in the store, but her heart was no longer in her work. She was so downcast that she didn't recognize the young woman who entered the store one evening. Mei saw the man first and didn't recognize him, so she wasn't expecting to recognize the woman. It was only when they approached the counter that she suddenly saw that it was Jadira. But this was a different Jadira than she had met before. There was no confidence in her eyes, no arrogance in her demeanor. Instead, Mei sensed fear.

"Hello Mei, do you remember me?"

"Yes, you are Jadira." Mei tried to smile, wondering what was coming next.

"This is my husband, Bolat," Jadira said, indicating the man standing beside her.

"And that is my husband, Gui," Mei said indicating her husband who was helping another customer.

Jadira nodded. "I was wondering if I could speak with you. Perhaps my husband and I could have some time with you and your husband?"

"Certainly." Mei nodded. "It is almost closing time. Do you want to talk now or sometime tomorrow?"

"No, let's talk tonight. I've been wanting to talk to you for some time now."

"Really?" Mei's eyes displayed her disbelief and fear edged her voice a little. She waited a moment until Gui's customer left and then introduced Gui to Bolat and Jadira.

"There is no one here now, and it is almost closing time." Gui smiled, "I will close the store and we can sit and have some tea."

Mei slipped behind the curtain to make tea and to also check on Huan, who was going to sleep. Then she returned and the two couples sat around a small kerosene heater, trying to keep warm as the winter wind blew outside.

Jadira spoke first. "I would like to tell you my story," she began. "I come from a good Muslim family. My father and mother were good Muslims, and I was raised to follow Allah. All my life, I have sought to please Allah. Since I was a little girl, I have prayed five times a day, plus I pray seventeen rotas, three times a day. Since I was a little girl, I read through the Qur'an once every ten days. Everyone around me respects me as a good Muslim."

Jadira paused, and Bolat smiled at her to encourage her. "My mother introduced me to the power of Islam. In Islam, speaking to the jinn is not forbidden. Jinn are simply spiritual beings that are all around us. My mother taught me how to obtain spiritual power from the spiritual realm. Whenever I prayed for people, they would get better. Whenever I cursed someone, they would get sick, or they would have an accident. I can even tell you what someone is doing in another room."

"All of this comes from the Qur'an. In the Qur'an there are words that are repeated continually. They have no meaning. They are the secrets of the Qur'an, and I learned how to use them. This was how I made my living. Bolat works also. But people pay me to use my spiritual powers. We have a good life. We own a nice home and we live well."

"But one day I met you." Jadira pointed an accusing finger at Mei. "And you prayed that I would lose my power. Ever since that day, I have been powerless. Nothing I do works." She paused. "I was angry with you. I wanted to contact my mother to put a curse on you. I was ready to go one day when a spirit entered the room. It was an evil jinn. I was filled with fear, and I used all the tools that Islam has for me. I commanded him to leave 'in the name of Allah.' I shouted, 'Satan I rebuke you!' but nothing worked. The jinn was too powerful. The jinn took me by the throat and started choking me. I was totally desperate. He was choking the life out of me; I was dying. I cried out to the heavens, 'Allah, help me.' Jadira looked up, her eyes wide. 'Immediately I heard a voice, as clear as you hear my voice today. The voice said, 'speak the name of Jesus.' I didn't think about it. I didn't wonder about it. I was desperate. I just used it.

"I cried out, 'Jesus if you are true, show me yourself.' I don't know why I worded it that way, but suddenly everything was back to normal. The demon was gone. I could breathe again. I didn't go and see my mother. I stayed home. I was so confused. I didn't understand what had happened."

Jadira was now shaking. Bolat put his hand on Jadira's shoulder to encourage her.

"This was the beginning of my confusion. Why would Jesus help a Muslim? I had done everything in my power to be a good Muslim. I had tried to go and make myself good in the ways of Allah. I was a Muslim. Why would Jesus help me?" Jadira paused. "I tried to forget about it. I tried to go about life normally, but the question would keep coming back to me…why would Jesus help a Muslim? I believe in Muhammad. He was the last prophet. Islam is the perfect religion. So why would Jesus help me?"

"I then decided to pray and fast and ask God to show me the right path. I know that the ways of Allah are many. No matter what path you take up the mountain, you get to the top. Perhaps God had a specific way for me. So, I prayed and fasted. I asked God, 'what is it you want me to do? What way should I follow you?' I prayed and fasted for two weeks. At the end of two weeks, I still had no answer. I had no chance of finding out what I wanted."

There were tears in Jadira's eyes. "I was so discouraged. At this point, I had no idea if God even existed. What was the use? I had tried to follow Allah. If he knew my heart, he would know that I loved him. I truly loved him and wanted to serve him. And now I had asked for two weeks, and there was nothing." Jadira looked defiant. "That was when I decided that I would forget religion. If Allah refused to answer me, then I was going to go do my own thing and please myself."

Jadira looked up at Mei. "Please don't be angry with me. Please believe me. This really happened. At that moment, I felt the power of God fill the room. It was very strange. In Islam, the greatest sin you can commit is 'doubting Allah.' And I had done it. I had doubted the teachings of Islam. I had doubted the prophet. I knew in my heart that Allah never visits human beings. Muhammad was the last one who heard from Allah, and that was through an angel. So there I was, when I had committed the greatest sin of Islam. Suddenly, I was confronted with the presence of God. And I felt something strange. He was so good and perfect. He was clean, and I was so dirty and defiled. I knew that because he is just, he must kill me; he must wipe me off the face of the earth. I cried. I didn't want to die. He was so pure, and I was so wicked. I curled up in a corner and cried out: god forgive me, God forgive me, forgive me, forgive me."

Tears were streaming down Jadira's face as she talked. "As I was crying, I felt the touch of God's hand on my shoulder and I heard him say: I forgive you. And the moment those words were spoken, I physically felt forgiven. Please don't think I am crazy," Jadira pleaded. "In Islam we don't know if we are forgiven until the day of judgment. Even Muhammad must wait like everyone else until the Day of judgment. So, who is this God who says,' I forgive you' and I feel forgiven?

"'Who are you?' I cried out. All he said was: I am the way, the truth and the life. I knew these words were of great importance. I wondered, 'Who is this God?' I couldn't look at him but I cried out again: what is your name? 'Jesus Christ the living God.' I started weeping…and weeping…and weeping."

By this time, Jadira was weeping again and could no longer speak. Her whole body shook. Bolat gently put his arm around his wife and held her. "What does this all mean?" he asked. "When you were at Rosa's house, you prayed in the name of Jesus. We came to you to learn more about Jesus." His voice cracked. "If Jadira is forgiven, I too want to be forgiven."

Mei was speechless. She felt so ashamed. Here she had been doubting. She had been so discouraged because nothing was happening. Everything she had done had come to nothing. God was building his kingdom, and she wasn't even aware of it. Tears ran down her own face. She was so thankful that Gui was there. She watched in amazement. He was so strong and so gentle. He had taken a Bible and had opened it to the gospel of John CHAPTER 14. Aloud he read:

Jesus said: "Do not let your hearts be troubled. Trust in God; trust also in me. In my Father's house are many rooms; if it were not so, I would have told you. I am going there to prepare a place for you. And if I go and prepare a place for you, I will come back and take you to be with me that you also may be where I am. You know the way to the place where I am going." Thomas said to him, "Lord, we don't know where you are going, so how can we know the way?" Jesus answered, "I am the way and the truth and the life. No one comes to the Father except through me."

Slowly and carefully Gui explained that Jesus was the way to heaven. Heaven was the place where God lived. And through Jesus we are offered the way to God. Jesus doesn't offer us paradise as Muhammad did, he offers us a way to God himself.

The two couples sat together for several hours discussing the scriptures. In the end Gui asked if he could pray with Bolat and Jadira. They were completely open to anything Gui had to say. Gui led them in a simple prayer, asking God to forgive them of their sin, and acknowledging Jesus as Lord of their lives. When they looked up, Bolat had tears streaming down his face. He didn't say much, he simple embraced Gui, and then Jadira looked at the clock. "Oh my," she gasped. "It is long after midnight." They soon excused themselves.

Gui and Mei looked at each other in amazement and then burst out laughing. They were so happy. This was all so unexpected, and yet it was what they had dreamed of for so long.

47

Over the next two weeks, Jadira and Bolat dropped by the store every day or two. They were reading the Bible together each night. Throughout the day, Jadira was reading book after book in the Bible. She was so excited about the things she found in the Bible that she would share them with Mei on their visits. One day, Rosa happened to come by the store when Jadira was talking excitedly about what she had read that day. Rosa looked very strangely at the two women. Then she smiled and came over to them with a very questioning look on her face. "Since when did you two become friends?"

Mei smiled shyly. Jadira came to her rescue. "I met Mei at your house the first time. Thank you for introducing her to me." Her eyes searched Rosas. "Mei and I have become good friends. We love to talk about God together."

"Really?" Rosa was incredulous. "I thought you two would be enemies."

"Mei has helped me understand many things about God. I've been reading the Bible and learning about Jesus."

Rosa's eyes were big. "This is so amazing," she said. "I've also been reading the Bible that Mei gave me, but I've never had the courage to ask questions."

"Really?" It was Mei's turn to be surprised. "You can come by anytime. Not that I know all the answers. But we can discuss them together."

"Can I change the subject?" Jadira asked. "Bolat wanted to know if you and Gui would like to come with us for a picnic this weekend. We will go out of the city and enjoy the countryside."

"That would be lovely," Mei smiled. "Huan longs to get out of the city. We would very much enjoy it."

"You and Erjan are invited too!" Jadira said, smiling at Rosa.

"Are you sure?" Rosa asked, not wanting to interrupt their plans, but secretly very happy to be invited as well. Soon the women were discussing plans for the weekend trip.

Several days later, the three couples and their children prepared the mini-bus that Bolat had borrowed for the day. They piled in their food, wood for making a fire, and blankets to sit on. Bolat had chosen a place with some trees where they would be protected from the wind and sun, and yet could look out over the barren countryside.

The three families enjoyed setting up their little camp and soon they had a fire going. The men sat around in one group and the women in another. After some time, Gui asked about the tents he could see in the distance. Bolat said that they belonged to nomads. Erjan and Bolat discussed nomads for a while and then they asked Gui if he would like to walk over and visit them. Gui was interested in learning about other people and the two boys were immediately interested as well, so the small group of men made their way across the barren ground towards the tents.

When they arrived at the small encampment, Bolat did most of the talking. He apparently knew several nomadic families, and he soon established who he was. The nomads then began showing the men around the camp, especially the horses and camels. One of the young men brought out a bowl and began milking a horse. Then he invited the men to sit in a circle. Gui had the opportunity to drink some of the mare's milk. Huan politely refused, and the men laughed. Huan, however, did not refuse the hot black tea that was offered afterward.

After drinking tea, the men walked back over the barren hills to where the women were waiting. Their meal was almost ready, so they sat again and enjoyed one another's company. Rosa was full of questions, wondering how Mei and Jadira had become such good friends.

Mei tried to answer, but Jadira interrupted her. "Let me tell," she said. "It is really my story." She paused, gathering her thoughts. "It all began when Mei prayed in Jesus' name that I would lose my power. Do you remember that day?" Rosa nodded and Jadira went on to tell her testimony. She ended by sharing how she had met with Jesus and experienced forgiveness.

Then Bolat spoke. "Jadira has always had special experiences. For me, it was different. I was just a good Muslim. I had no special powers and didn't really want any. I was more interested in making money and enjoying life. But when Jadira experienced forgiveness from Jesus, she became a different woman. Suddenly, she was everything I had ever wanted. I don't mean that in a physical way. I've always loved Jadira, but suddenly she was different. She was kind and considerate and gentle. It was like she was a new woman. So I suggested that we search out Mei and try and learn more about this Jesus." Bolat paused and then went on to explain how he had also found forgiveness.

Erjan and Rosa nodded as the story was told. Rosa was keenly aware that Erjan was interested and open to discussing these things. The two boys had moved off to the edge of the trees, talking with each other, so the adults were left to themselves. Bolat then urged Erjan to pray to Jesus for forgiveness and cleansing. Gui watched in amazement as his friend quietly said, "I would like to, but I don't know how."

Bolat turned to Gui. "You tell him, just as you told me."

"I would like to pray too," Rosa said, blushing when Erjan's eyes met hers. Tears of joy slipped down Mei's face as the small group bowed their heads in prayer.

48

It was a happy occasion when the three couples met at Erjan and Rosa's home for their first church service. Mei and Gui were nervous about the meeting, but the other two couples were eager to learn how to worship God. Gui, Mei and Huan began by teaching them two simple worship songs. Jadira was very surprised. "I didn't think a person could sing religious songs. Singing is only about secular things, guys and girls and that sort of thing."

"God gave us music to enjoy. That means that he also enjoys music. The Bible has many examples where people sang in worship. It also talks about how we can experience a closeness to God in worship. Several of the prophets desired music to be played while they sought God," Mei explained.

The small group sang the worship songs several times and Mei promised to teach them more songs the next week. Then they asked each other for prayer requests so they could pray for one another. As they went around the group, most of the requests were about members of their families with whom they wanted to share their newfound faith.

However, when they came to Rosa, she blushed and looked down. "I'm not sure how to say this, but I was wondering if you could pray for me. I wish that I could enjoy the Bible like Jadira does. She reads all day. But when I try to read the Bible, I fall asleep. When I fight to stay awake, I start to shake all over."

Erjan looked concerned as tears ran down his wife's cheeks. He looked over at Gui who was unsure what to say. It was Mei who answered.

"I think this is the work of the enemy, trying to keep you from reading God's word." She looked at the others. "I think we should pray for Rosa that she would be set free from this." They all nodded. "I think we should also pray for this house."

"What do you mean?" Jadira asked. "How do you pray for a house?"

"Let's walk from room to room and ask God to take control of the house. Let's give every room to him and ask him to become Lord of the house and ask him to keep the enemy out of this home. When Rosa and Erjan come home every day, this house should be a protected holy place where they are safe from any attacks of the enemy."

"I didn't know we could do that," Jadira cried out. "When we are done here, can you come over and pray for my house? I want my house blessed as well."

Soon the three couples were moving from room to room, asking that God would fill Rosa's and Erjan's house with his presence, and protect them from the attacks of the evil one. They blessed the house and asked for God's protection over it. After the prayer time, Gui led them in a simple Bible study on understanding the Bible. When they finished, Jadira insisted that they also come to her house that very night to pray over it. It was a joyful occasion as the three couples prayed and committed Bolat and Jadira's house to the Lord.

That night, after Huan had gone to sleep, Mei and Gui held tightly onto each other and prayed together. Mei was so happy. She had never imagined that God would give them two other couples who were so committed to following Jesus. She never imagined that she would feel so blessed and fulfilled in her ministry. Gui at the same time was praising God for Huan's friend Askar. Earlier that day, Erjan had announced that Askar was no longer going to take Islamic lessons at the mosque. Instead, the two fathers and two boys would read and study the Bible together. As Gui held his wife close, he wondered what other wonderful things God had in store for them. Only time would tell.

The End

www.ingramcontent.com/pod-product-compliance
Lightning Source LLC
Chambersburg PA
CBHW030442090526
44586CB00044B/519